Helping our Youngest to Learn and Grow

POLICIES FOR EARLY LEARNING

This work is published under the responsibility of the Secretary-General of the OECD. The opinions expressed and arguments employed herein do not necessarily reflect the official views of the OECD member countries.

This document, as well as any data and any map included herein, are without prejudice to the status of or sovereignty over any territory, to the delimitation of international frontiers and boundaries and to the name of any territory, city or area.

Please cite this publication as:
Andreas Schleicher (2019), *Helping our Youngest to Learn and Grow: Policies for Early Learning*, International Summit on the Teaching Profession, OECD Publishing, Paris.
http://dx.doi.org/10.1787/9789264313873-en

ISBN 978-92-64-31386-6 (print)
ISBN 978-92-64-31387-3 (PDF)
ISBN 978-92-64-78919-7 (ePub)
ISBN 978-92-64-88956-9 (HTML)

Series: International Summit on the Teaching Profession
ISSN 2312-7082 (print)
ISSN 2312-7090 (online)

The statistical data for Israel are supplied by and under the responsibility of the relevant Israeli authorities. The use of such data by the OECD is without prejudice to the status of the Golan Heights, East Jerusalem and Israeli settlements in the West Bank under the terms of international law.

Photo credits:
© Diego Cervo / Shutterstock
© Monkey Business Images / Shutterstock

Foreword

In March 2019, the Finnish Ministry of Education, the OECD, and Education International brought education ministers, union leaders and other teacher leaders together for the International Summit on the Teaching Profession with the aim to better support the teaching profession in meeting the formidable challenges of 21st-century education.

One of the secrets of the success of the International Summit on the Teaching Profession is that it explores difficult and controversial issues on the basis of sound evidence, provided by the OECD as the global leader for internationally comparative data and analysis. For the first time, the Summit focused on early childhood education and care. This report summarises evidence that can underpin the discussion of this topic.

The first five years of a child's life are critical to his or her development. During this period, children learn at a faster rate than at any other time in their lives, developing cognitive, and social and emotional skills that are fundamental to their achievements throughout childhood and as adults. The rapid pace of development in early childhood means that investing in young children, both through their families and through access to high-quality early childhood education and care, leads to strong personal, social and economic returns. Effective early learning also predicts positive well-being across a range of indicators in adulthood, including general well-being, physical and mental health, educational attainment and employment. Disadvantaged children benefit from quality early childhood education and care the most, so investing in early childhood education and care and improving the quality of the environment for early development and learning could boost social mobility and inclusive growth.

While most countries have clearly articulated curricula and well-established pedagogical approaches when it comes to primary and upper secondary education, there is much less agreement among and within countries on how best to build strong foundations in early childhood education and care in order to shift the emphasis from access to quality, and from care to quality education. There is also much debate over age-appropriate pedagogies and the right balance in the development of cognitive, and social and emotional competencies. Often the provision of early childhood education and care is highly fragmented within education systems.

All of this has major implications for the initial and continued professional development of staff, and for the work organisation and governance of early childhood education and care.

Following an introductory chapter on policy challenges facing early childhood education and care, the second chapter of this report examines structural and process quality in early childhood education and care, issues that are closely related to policy design and implementation, and to dialogue between government and the profession. The third chapter then turns to what happens inside early childhood institutions with a review of pedagogical practice and the policies that can shape it. Both of these chapters are based on the OECD Starting Strong projects and related publications (main authors: Clara Barata, Eric Charbonnier, Arno Engel, Victoria Liberatore, Ineke Litjens, Elizabeth Shuey, Megan Sim, Miho Taguma and Stephanie Wall) and on findings from the PISA 2015 assessment (main authors: Francesco Avvisati, Alfonso Echazarra, Carlos Gonzáles-Sancho and Mario Piacentini).

One of the topics that policy makers, educators and parents struggle most with these days concerns understanding the merits and demerits of introducing technology to foster children's development. The rise in the amount of time children spend in front of screens has led to concerns about the consequences of technology use, and how it may affect children's brains and their socio-emotional, cognitive and physical development. The fourth chapter explores the interplay between technology and learning, and summarises some of the literature on the effects of technology use on children, based on

a working paper prepared by Francesca Gottschalk. A final section on the role of schools and policy in safe Internet use is drawn from a working paper prepared by Julie Hooft Graafland.

The report was prepared by Andreas Schleicher with input from Yuri Belfali and Karine Tremblay, and with support from Marilyn Achiron.

Andreas Schleicher
Director for Education and Skills and Special Advisor
on Education Policy to the Secretary-General

Table of Contents

Follow OECD Publications on:

http://twitter.com/OECD_Pubs

http://www.facebook.com/OECDPublications

http://www.linkedin.com/groups/OECD-Publications-4645871

http://www.youtube.com/oecdilibrary

http://www.oecd.org/oecddirect/

This book has...

StatLinks

A service that delivers Excel® files from the printed page!

Look for the *StatLinks* at the bottom of the tables or graphs in this book. To download the matching Excel® spreadsheet, just type the link into your Internet browser, starting with the *http://dx.doi.org* prefix, or click on the link from the e-book edition.

Executive Summary

Research has shown that attendance at early childhood education and care programmes can have a significant impact on children's cognitive, social and emotional development, and on their performance in school – and in life – later on. There is evidence from both randomised controlled trials and observational studies that early childhood education and care has the potential to improve the life chances of children from disadvantaged families; yet results from PISA show that advantaged children are more likely to attend, and to attend for longer periods of time. Failing to tackle this situation could mean that early childhood education and care continue to exacerbate rather than mitigate inequities in education and in society.

Some evidence suggests that peers in early childhood education and care influence children's language and socio-emotional development. It is thus urgent for policy makers to identify the extent to which disadvantaged children are clustered together in early childhood education and care programmes, and whether and where centres with substantial numbers of disadvantaged children are of lower quality than those attended by more affluent children. In most countries, socio-economically disadvantaged children are the least likely to attend high-quality programmes.

WHAT ARE THE INGREDIENTS OF QUALITY EARLY CHILDHOOD EDUCATION AND CARE?

A growing body of research suggests that the magnitude of the benefits of early childhood education and care depends on the quality of the services provided. Quality in this context depends on both the infrastructure, i.e. the available physical, human and material resources, and what is known as "process quality", i.e. the social, emotional and instructional aspects of children's interactions with staff members and other children. In order to attract the most suitable candidates to the early learning workforce, countries need not only to offer adequate pay, but also provide an environment where leaders and other staff are given the autonomy, and have the time and space to work as professionals.

Although research emphasises the importance of initial education and continuous professional development opportunities for early learning staff, there is no simple relationship between the staff's level of education and process quality or children's learning, development and well-being. One way to improve the pedagogical practices used in these programmes is to enhance the staff's competence to communicate and interact with children in a shared and sustainable manner. Research finds that it is not necessary for all staff to have attained high levels of education. Highly qualified staff can have a positive influence on colleagues who work with them but who do not have the same level of qualifications.

WHICH PEDAGOGIES WORK BEST FOR THE YOUNGEST LEARNERS?

A distinction is often drawn between child-centred instruction (activities are child-initiated, children engage in problem solving and enquiry-oriented learning) and didactic instruction (staff-directed, planned tasks focusing on acquiring and practicing academic skills). Both approaches may boost children's skills and practitioners could combine different approaches depending on the purpose; but some evidence suggests the importance of including child-centred instruction at the earliest ages. Research shows that academic, staff-initiated practices and approaches are more likely to improve children's academic outcomes, including IQ scores, literacy and numeracy skills, and specific subject knowledge, while child-centred practices are more likely to improve a child's socio-emotional and soft skills, such as motivation to learn, creativity, independence, self-confidence, general knowledge and initiative. Research also cautions that strong, didactic, staff-directed practices may hinder the development of children's socio-emotional skills, such as motivation, interest and self-regulation, in the long run.

The curricula for early childhood education and care often contrast with those used in primary schooling, partly because the latter tend to focus on the content to be taught, while the former typically rely on psychological and educational theories that inform pedagogical practice, i.e. how to teach, rather than what to teach. While pedagogy is something that

happens in staff-child interactions, policy can shape pedagogical environments, for example, through curriculum design, through initial and continuing staff development, and through work organisation.

An OECD study shows that almost all countries have some form of national-level curriculum or framework in place for early learning. The prescribed learning areas and goals of this framework/curriculum influence the pedagogical approaches and practices used by early childhood education and care providers. Public policy can also facilitate children's transition from early childhood education and care to primary school. Well-managed transitions support children's well-being, ensure that the benefits of early childhood education and care endure, prepare children for school and for life, and improve equity in education outcomes.

WHAT DO WE KNOW ABOUT CHILDREN'S USE OF TECHNOLOGY?

These days, preschoolers can become familiar with digital devices before they are exposed to books. Today, not only schools, but early childhood educational institutions too are exploring ways to integrate information and communication technology (ICT) into the learning environment. Education systems need to re-evaluate their curricula, and teachers need to reassess their teaching styles, to ensure that ICT is used effectively. Education policies that foster the development of children's digital skills are those that provide adequate training for teachers, and support the integration of technologies into school curricula. Linking the way children interact with ICT inside of school to the way they already use it outside of school can be a key to unlocking technology's potential for learning.

At the same time, given the ubiquity of technology in the lives of 21st-century children, a concerted effort needs to be made to protect children from the risks associated with technology use. This includes educators, parents and health practitioners assessing whether screen time is affecting engagement in certain healthy behaviours (e.g. physical activity, regular meal-times, sleep), setting certain limits to screen use (i.e. limiting the use of certain devices close to bedtime) and ensuring content-appropriate programming for younger children and adolescents. Based on state-of-the-art evidence, the effects of technology on well-being are generally too small to warrant widespread policy change.

Chapter 1

POLICIES FOR EARLY LEARNING: PROVIDING EQUITABLE ACCESS

Research has shown that attendance at high-quality early childhood education and care programmes can have a significant impact on children's cognitive, social and emotional development, and on their performance in school later on. This chapter discusses how these programmes can also help reduce social inequalities and be particularly beneficial to disadvantaged children.

The first five years of a child's life are critical to his or her development. During this period, children learn at a faster rate than at any other time in their lives, developing cognitive, and social and emotional skills that are fundamental to their achievements throughout childhood and as adults.

Some effects of quality early childhood education and care on children's development and learning have been established in the literature, and there is a general consensus that the quality of education and care provided has a strong impact on children's early development (Melhuish et al., 2015[1]). The OECD Starting Strong reports (OECD, 2001[2]; OECD, 2006[3]; OECD, 2011[4]; OECD, 2015[5]; OECD, 2017[6]) and other international research point out that high-quality early childhood education and care is beneficial for children's early development and their subsequent school performance in language use and emerging academic skills, early literacy and numeracy, and socio-emotional skills (Burchinal, 2016[7]; Cappella, Aber and Kim, 2016[8]; Melhuish et al., 2015[1]; Yoshikawa and Kabay, 2015[9]). In addition, the OECD Programme for International Student Assessment, or PISA, shows that 15-year-old students who had attended early childhood education for one year or longer are significantly more likely than students who had attended such a programme for less than one year to attain the baseline level of proficiency in reading, mathematics and science (OECD, 2017[10]).

Box 1.1. Definitions of terms used in this report

Early childhood education and care includes all arrangements providing care and education for children under compulsory school age, regardless of setting, funding, opening hours or programme content.

Pre-primary education refers to services for children to support early development in preparation for participation in school and society, accommodating children from age three to the start of primary education. It is also often referred to as "preschool" and it corresponds to ISCED level 0.2. For international comparability purposes, the term "early childhood education" is used to label ISCED level 0.

The benefits of high-quality early childhood education and care also extend to health and well-being, for example by helping instil the habits of eating healthily and doing regular physical activity (OECD, 2014[11]). Evidence is growing that high-quality early childhood education and care services also help support children's outcomes later in life, as manifested in greater labour market participation, a reduction in the incidence of poverty, greater inter-generational social mobility and better social integration (Sammons et al., 2008[12]; Sylva et al., 2004[13]).

An early learning environment that provides children with opportunities to engage in developmentally appropriate, stimulating and language-rich activities, and social interactions can compensate for the risks for children from disadvantaged backgrounds of falling behind or not reaching their full potential (Arnold and Doctoroff, 2003[14]; Heckman, 2006[15]). Research highlights the long-term benefits of investments in early childhood education and care programmes.

Effective early learning also predicts well-being in adulthood across a range of indicators, including general well-being, physical and mental health, educational attainment and employment. The areas of early learning that are of particular importance for many adult outcomes include: language and literacy; numeracy and other non-verbal cognitive skills; self-regulation; emotional health; social well-being; and social and emotional skills. During early learning, gains in one domain contribute to gains in others. This cycle of reinforcement across domains means that early learning programmes should be assessed using a whole-child approach, recognising the overlapping nature of outcomes for young children.

A key goal of most governments' attempts to increase access to early childhood education and care is to improve equity in outcomes for older children and adults. This objective is also reflected in United Nations Sustainable Development Goal 4.2: "Ensure that all children have access to quality early childhood education and care so that they are ready for primary education."

Box 1.2. Sustainable Development Goal 4.2

Sustainable Development Goal 4 has 10 targets encompassing many different aspects of education. Seven of these targets are expected outcomes; three are the means of achieving these targets. Goal 4.2 specifically focuses on early childhood.

SDG target 4.2 Early childhood development and universal pre-primary education

By 2030, ensure that all girls and boys have access to quality early childhood development, care and pre-primary education so that they are ready for primary education.

Indicator 4.2.1: The proportion of children under 5 years of age who are developmentally on track in health, learning and psychosocial well-being, by sex

Indicator 4.2.2: The participation rate in organised learning (one year before the official primary age), by sex

---

ATTENDANCE AT EARLY CHILDHOOD EDUCATION AND CARE AND LEARNING OUTCOMES

To reap the benefits of early childhood education and care, children must attend a programme. Many of the inequalities observed in school systems are already present when students first enter formal schooling and persist as students progress through education. Because research shows that inequalities tend to grow the longer students are enrolled in school, early childhood education and care can reduce inequalities in education – as long as participation is universal and the learning opportunities are consistently of high quality.

Access to early childhood education and care has risen sharply in OECD countries, and there is a growing awareness of the importance of educational and pedagogical programmes for very young children. Despite the increase in recent years, enrolment rates remain low for younger children, especially for those under the age of three. On average across OECD countries, about 35% of children under three were enrolled in early childhood education and care programmes in 2016, although participation at this age varies significantly across countries. By contrast, for the vast majority of OECD countries, more than 90% of five-year-olds are enrolled (Figure 1.1). These countries are already close to or have reached the Sustainable Development Goal's target of universal participation in organised learning one year before the official age at entry into primary education.

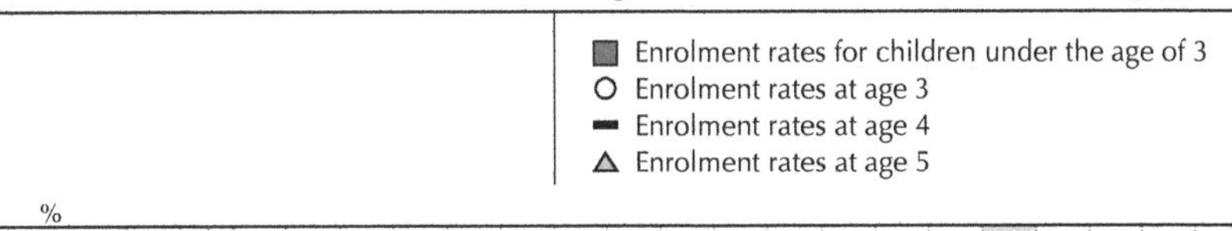

Figure 1.1

Enrolment rates in early childhood education and primary education, by age

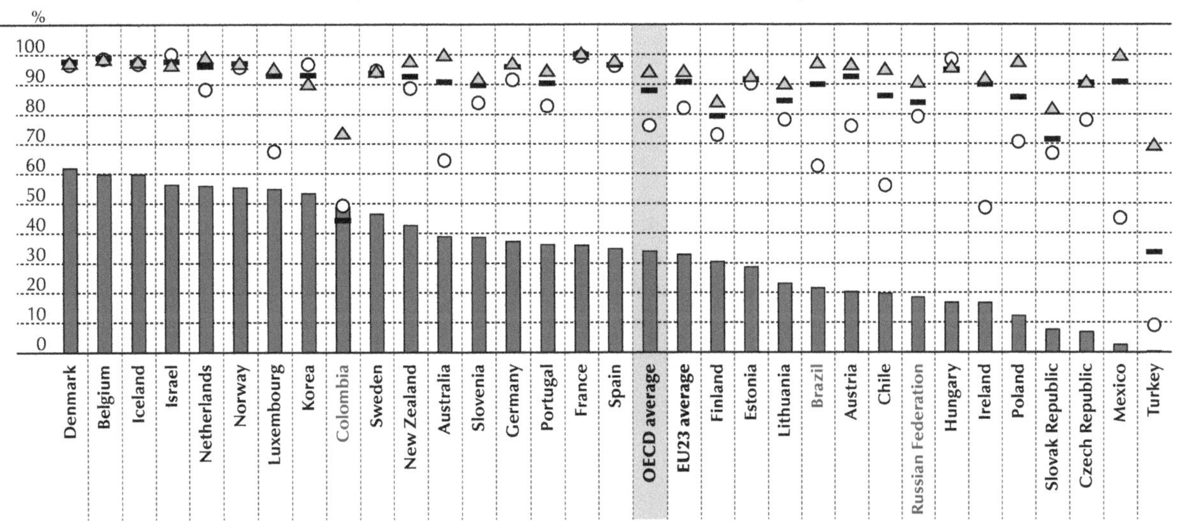

Note: Children under the age of 3 are enrolled in formal childcare (ISCED 0 and other registered early childhood education and care services); 4- and 5-year-old children may already be enrolled in primary education in some countries.
Source: OECD (2018), *Education at a Glance 2018: OECD Indicators*, OECD Publishing, Paris, https://dx.doi.org/10.1787/eag-2018-en.

The increase in access is partly the result of extensions of legal entitlements to a place in such programmes for children under the age of three, and of efforts to ensure free access for 3-5 year-olds. However, significant differences persist across OECD countries in the quality of the programmes offered and in the usual number of hours per week that each child is enrolled. Access is not a guarantee of high-quality early childhood education and care. Therefore, in many countries, the curriculum framework for pre-primary education has been extended to enhance the quality of those programmes and to ensure a better transition between pre-primary and primary education.

PISA 2015 found that 15-year-old students score four points higher in science for every additional year they had spent in pre-primary education; but the association largely disappears after accounting for the socio-economic status of students and schools. One reason why the association is weak, even before accounting for the socio-economic profile of students and schools, is that the relation is curvilinear: students who had spent less than one year in pre-primary education score lower in science than students who had not attended at all or who had spent more than one year.

EQUITY IN ACCESS TO EARLY CHILDHOOD EDUCATION AND LEARNING OUTCOMES

While students who had attended early childhood education and care programmes for longer scored better in PISA, on average across countries, the benefits are significantly greater for socio-economically disadvantaged children (as shown in Figures 1.2 and 1.4). Failure to address these differences could mean that early childhood education and care exacerbates rather than mitigates inequity.

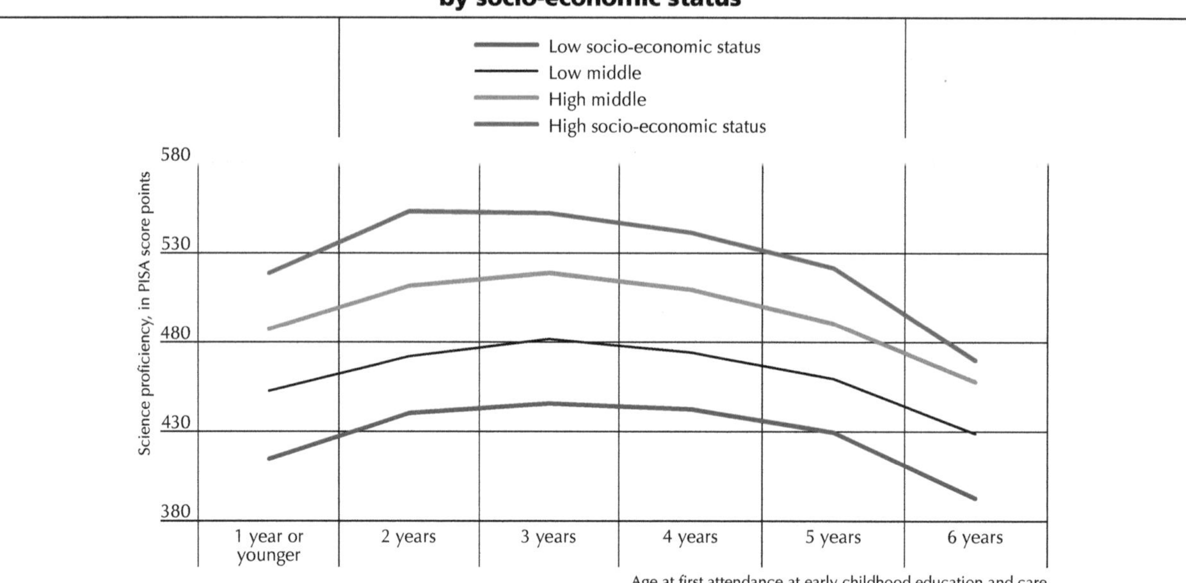

Figure 1.2

Age at starting early childhood education and care, and science proficiency at 15, by socio-economic status

Source: OECD, Programme for International Student Assessment (PISA) database, http://www.oecd.org/pisa/data/.

Across OECD countries, the average duration of attendance at early childhood education and care programmes is associated with certain characteristics of the schools 15-year-old students attend. Specifically, schools that serve a larger proportion of socio-economically advantaged students, private schools and schools in urban areas tend to have students who participated in early childhood education and care for a longer time than schools that serve fewer advantaged students, public schools and schools in rural areas, respectively (Figure 1.3). This suggests that participation in early childhood education and care is associated with a number of factors – including characteristics of the secondary schools students attend later on – that can also contribute to students' outcomes.

On average among 15-year-old students who remember their attendance at early childhood education (ISCED 0), 92% of them reported in PISA 2015 that they had attended early childhood education for "at least one year" and 77% of them reported they had attended for "at least two years". However, as noted above, in most countries, advantaged 15-year-old students had more opportunities than disadvantaged students to attend early childhood education. For instance, an average of 72% of disadvantaged 15-year-old students compared to 82% of advantaged students had attended early

childhood education for at least two years (Figure 1.4). Across OECD countries, the differences between the percentages of advantaged and disadvantaged students who had attended early childhood education and care for at least two years were larger than 18 percentage points in Slovenia, the Slovak Republic, Turkey and the United States. This means that the 15-years-old students who could have benefited the most from early childhood education – those from disadvantaged backgrounds – were less likely to have participated in those kinds of programmes when they were younger.

Figure 1.3

Differences in duration of attendance at early childhood education and care, by school characteristics

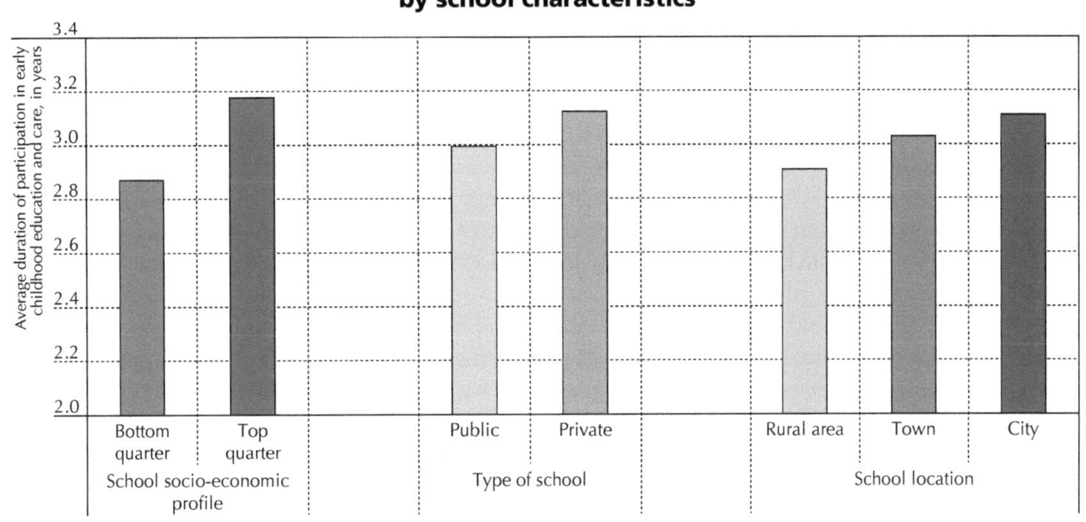

Source: OECD, Programme for International Student Assessment (PISA) database, http://www.oecd.org/pisa/data/.

Figure 1.4

Percentage of 15-year-old students who had attended preschool for two years or more, by socio-economic status (2015)

Early childhood education (ISCED 0)

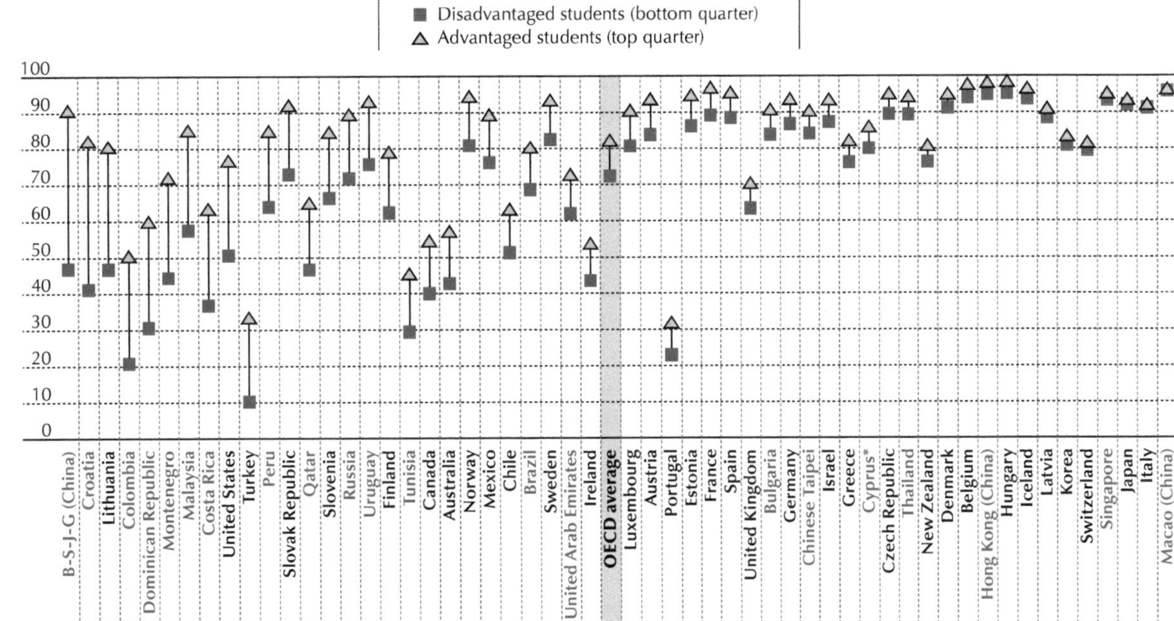

*See notes at the beginning of this chapter.
Note: B-S-J-G (China) refers to Beijing-Shanghai-Jiangsu-Guangdong (China).
Countries and economies are ranked in descending order of the difference between the percentages of socio-economically advantaged and disadvantaged students who had attended early childhood education and care for two years or more.
Source: OECD (2017), *Starting Strong 2017: Key OECD Indicators on Early Childhood Education and Care*, OECD Publishing, Paris, http://dx.doi.org/10.1787/9789264276116-3-en. OECD, Programme for International Student Assessment (PISA) database, http://www.oecd.org/pisa/data/.

Similar inequities are observed when rural schools and urban schools, or public and private schools are compared. Across OECD countries, 15-year-old students in urban schools had spent two months more in early childhood education than students enrolled in rural schools; 15-year-olds students enrolled in private schools had also spent two months more in early childhood education than students enrolled in public schools (OECD, 2016[16]).

Early childhood education and care programmes are especially important for students with an immigrant background. They can help develop the linguistic and social skills needed to integrate in a new country's school system. Immigrant students who reported that they had attended early childhood education and care programmes scored 49 points higher, on average, on the PISA reading assessment than those who had not participated in such programmes – the equivalent of around one-and-a-half additional years of schooling. Moreover, PISA data show that immigrant students benefit more, academically, over the long term than native students when they enrol in early childhood education and care at a younger age. As 15-year-olds, they even score higher than native-born students on the PISA science assessment.

ADDRESSING SOCIAL INEQUALITY THROUGH EARLY CHILDHOOD EDUCATION AND CARE

The early childhood education and care literature has traditionally focused specifically on socio-economic differences and the potential of high-quality early childhood education and care to compensate for deprived home environments, see for recent overviews (Duncan and Magnuson, 2013[17]; Leseman and Slot, 2014[18]). For instance, preventing "intellectual disability" among poor children was the main focus of renown early-intervention studies, such as the Perry Preschool (Schweinhart and Weikart, 1997[19]). The main idea, which remains dominant in both research papers and policy documents, is that if children are exposed to a safe, nurturing and enriching environment in early childhood education and care, their experiences in this environment will offset the negative effects associated with poverty. There is evidence from both randomised controlled trials and observational studies that early childhood education and care has the potential to improve the life chances of children from disadvantaged families (Barnett, 2011[20]; Camilli et al., 2010[21]; Dearing, McCartney and Taylor, 2009[22]; Melhuish et al., 2008[23]; Zachrisson and Dearing, 2014[24]).

It is therefore a paradox that, with a few exceptions, across countries there is social selection into early childhood education and care, and differences in the quality of that education and care, with socio-economically disadvantaged children being the least likely to attend high-quality programmes (Petitclerc et al., 2017[25]). This includes countries with market-based and targeted programmes, e.g. in the United States (Fuller, Holloway and Liang, 1996[26]) and countries with subsidised universal access to early childhood education and care, such as Norway (Sibley et al., 2015[27]; Zachrisson, Janson and Nærde, 2013[28]) .

Moreover, although the cited studies show that attending (compared to not attending) high-quality early childhood education and care programmes may benefit children's development, well-being and learning, it remains an open question as to what constitutes the "active ingredients" or the quality features responsible for these outcomes (Duncan and Magnuson, 2013[17]; Sim et al., 2018[29]). For instance, two meta-analyses of the process quality of staff-child interactions failed to find that quality to be more beneficial for disadvantaged than for advantaged children (Keys et al., 2013[30]). Identifying disparities related to socio-economic status in the quality of early childhood education and care (broadly defined) and disentangling the "active ingredients" involved in promoting equity in developmental opportunities should therefore be priorities in future research (Duncan and Magnuson, 2013[17]; Sim et al., 2018[29]).

Children from disadvantaged families, and from ethnically diverse families, often attend centres with other children from similar backgrounds (Becker and Schober, 2017[31]). Merging evidence from the United States and Norway suggests that peers in early childhood education and care influence both language and socio-emotional development (Justice et al., 2011[32]; Neidell and Waldfogel, 2010[33]; Ribeiro and Zachrisson, 2017[34]; Ribeiro, Zachrisson and Dearing, 2017[35]). Thus, the composition of the peer group influences children's development. For example, a study from the United States found children to develop better cognitive school-readiness skills when attending preschool with children of higher average socio-economic status, regardless of the child's own background (Reid and Ready, 2013[36]). Likewise, in the Netherlands, children from disadvantaged families who attended programmes with children from a variety of backgrounds gained more in literacy and reading skills than children in socio-economically homogeneous groups (de Haan, A. et al., 2013[37]). In Germany, structural features and the availability of learning material was not associated with group composition (Becker and Schober, 2017[31]); but evidence from the United States suggests that in some contexts, parents in disadvantaged families tend to choose centres of lower quality than those chosen by more affluent parents (Dowsett et al., 2008[38]). It is therefore of high policy relevance to identify across countries the extent to which disadvantaged children are clustered together in early childhood education and care programmes, and whether and where centres with substantial numbers of disadvantaged children are of lower quality than centres attended by more affluent children.

Box 1.3. **International Early Learning and Child Well-being Study**

The International Early Learning and Child Well-being Study is designed to help countries improve children's early learning experiences in order to better support children's development and overall well-being. The study provides countries with a common language and framework to foster growing interest in and commitments to early childhood development. By collecting robust empirical information on children's early learning environments at home and on their early childhood education and care experiences, countries can identify factors that promote or hinder children's early learning. The knowledge generated by the study will be shared across countries and encourage countries to take action with the aim of improving children's outcomes and overall well-being. The study is led by the Organisation for Economic Co-operation and Development (OECD) with support from member governments and an international consortium of early childhood and research experts.

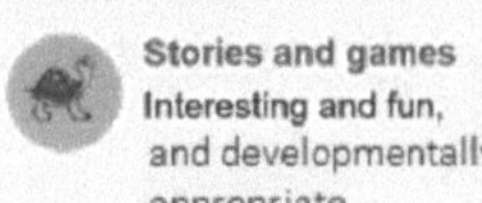

The study involves five-year-old children, their parents and teachers from early childhood education and care centres or schools, as well as trained study administrators. Ensuring the well-being of the children is the first priority of the study. For this reason, new tools for data collection were developed specifically with children in mind. Custom-made activities were created involving stories and games that are interesting, fun and developmentally appropriate for five-year-olds. The study takes a holistic approach and includes multiple domains of early learning: emergent cognitive skills, such as literacy and numeracy; social and emotional skills, such as empathy and trust; and skills that draw from both cognitive and non-cognitive capacities, such as self-regulation. In addition to including a comprehensive set of learning domains, the study collects information from a wide range of sources; children, parents, staff and study administrators provide information about children's emergent skills.

Launched in 2016, the study is one of the most ambitious international efforts to develop a comprehensive set of metrics around children's early learning. The results from the field trial in 2017 showed that children enjoy the animated stories and games, and that teachers and centre staff support an international focus on children's development at this age. Results from the study will be available in early 2020.

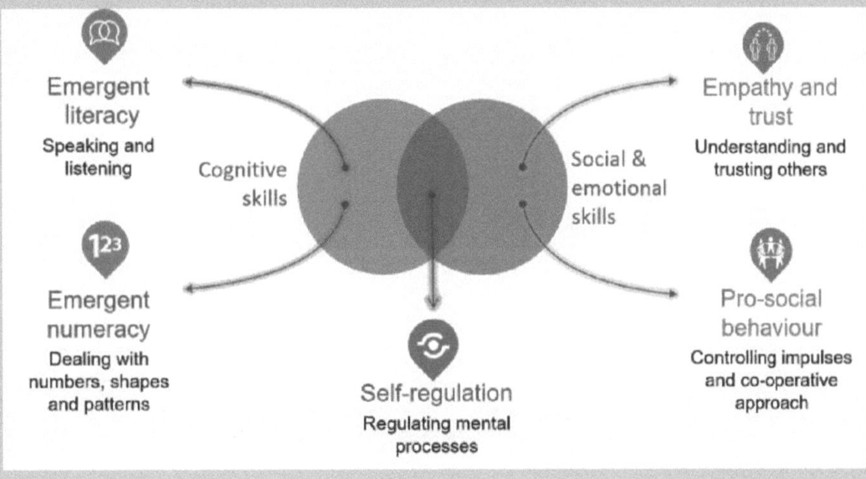

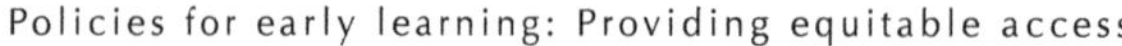

CONCLUSIONS

During the first five years of their life, children learn at a faster rate than at any other time, developing the cognitive, and social and emotional skills that are fundamental to their achievements throughout childhood and as adults. Early childhood education and care is thus a powerful lever to help children realise their potential.

Moreover, if children are exposed to a safe, nurturing and enriching environment in early childhood education and care, their experiences in these programmes can offset the negative consequences associated with disadvantage. There is evidence from both randomised controlled trials and observational studies that early childhood education and care has the potential to improve the life chances of children from disadvantaged families.

It is therefore a paradox that, across countries, there is consistent social selection into early childhood education and care, and differences in the quality of that education and care. Failure to address these differences could mean that early childhood education and care exacerbates rather than mitigates inequity. The next two chapters will examine policy options to address this issue.

References

Arnold, D. and G. Doctoroff (2003), "The early education of socioeconomically disadvantaged children", *Annual Review of Psychology*, Vol. 54/1, pp. 517-545, http://dx.doi.org/10.1146/annurev.psych.54.111301.145442. [14]

Barnett, W. (2011), "Effectiveness of Early Educational Intervention", *Science*, Vol. 333/6045, pp. 975-978, http://dx.doi.org/10.1126/science.1204534. [20]

Becker, B. and P. Schober (2017), "Not Just Any Child Care Center? Social and Ethnic Disparities in the Use of Early Education Institutions With a Beneficial Learning Environment", *Early Education and Development*, Vol. 28/8, pp. 1011-1034, http://dx.doi.org/10.1080/10409289.2017.1320900. [31]

Burchinal, E. (2016), "Quality, thresholds, features and dosage in early care and education: Secondary data analyses of child outcomes", *Monographs of the Society for Research in Child Development*, Vol. 81/2, http://dx.doi.org/10.1111/mono.12248. [7]

Camilli, G. et al. (2010), "Meta-analysis of the effects of early education interventions on cognitive and social development", *Teachers College Record*, Vol. 112/3, pp. 579–620. [21]

Cappella, E., J. Aber and H. Kim (2016), *Teaching Beyond Achievement Tests: Perspectives From Developmental and Education Science*, American Educational Research Association, http://dx.doi.org/10.3102/978-0-935302-48-6_4. [8]

de Haan, A. et al. (2013), "Targeted versus mixed preschools and kindergartens: Effects of class composition and teacher-managed activities on disadvanged children's emergent academic skills", *School Effectiveness and School Improvement: An International Journal of Research, Policy and Practice*, Vol. 24/2, pp. 177-194, http://dx.doi.org/10.1080/09243453.2012.749792. [37]

Dearing, E., K. McCartney and B. Taylor (2009), "Does Higher Quality Early Child Care Promote Low-Income Children's Math and Reading Achievement in Middle Childhood?", *Child Development*, Vol. 80/5, pp. 1329-1349, http://dx.doi.org/10.1111/j.1467-8624.2009.01336.x. [22]

Dowsett, C. et al. (2008), "Structural and process features in three types of child care for children from high and low income families", *Early Childhood Research Quarterly*, Vol. 23/1, pp. 69-93, http://dx.doi.org/10.1016/j.ecresq.2007.06.003. [38]

Duncan, G. and K. Magnuson (2013), "Investing in Preschool Programs", *Journal of Economic Perspectives*, Vol. 27/2, pp. 109-132, http://dx.doi.org/10.1257/jep.27.2.109. [17]

Fuller, B., S. Holloway and X. Liang (1996), "Family Selection of Child-Care Centers: The Influence of Household Support, Ethnicity, and Parental Practices", *Child Development*, Vol. 67/6, p. 3320, http://dx.doi.org/10.2307/1131781. [26]

Heckman, J. (2006), "Skill formation and the economics of investing in disadvantaged children", *Science*, Vol. 312/5782, pp. 1900-1902, http://dx.doi.org/10.1126/science.1128898. [15]

Justice, L. et al. (2011), "Peer Effects in Preschool Classrooms: Is Children's Language Growth Associated With Their Classmates' Skills?", *Child Development*, Vol. 82/6, pp. 1768-1777, http://www.jstor.org/stable/41289881. [32]

Keys, T. et al. (2013), "Preschool Center Quality and School Readiness: Quality Effects and Variation by Demographic and Child Characteristics", *Child Development*, Vol. 84/4, pp. 1171-1190, http://dx.doi.org/10.1111/cdev.12048. [30]

Leseman, P. and P. Slot (2014), "Breaking the cycle of poverty: challenges for European early childhood education and care", *European Early Childhood Education Research Journal*, Vol. 22/3, pp. 314-326, http://dx.doi.org/10.1080/1350293x.2014.912894. [18]

Melhuish, E. et al. (2015), *A review of research on the effects of early childhood education and care (ECEC) upon child development. WP4.1 Curriculum and quality analysis impact review*, CARE, http://ecec-care.org/fileadmin/careproject/Publications/reports/. [1]

Melhuish, E. et al. (2008), "THE EARLY YEARS: Preschool Influences on Mathematics Achievement", *Science*, Vol. 321/5893, pp. 1161-1162, http://dx.doi.org/10.1126/science.1158808. [23]

Neidell, M. and J. Waldfogel (2010), "Cognitive and Noncognitive Peer Effects in Early Education", *Review of Economics and Statistics*, Vol. 92/3, pp. 562-576, http://dx.doi.org/10.1162/rest_a_00012. [33]

OECD (2017), *Starting Strong 2017: Key OECD Indicators on Early Childhood Education and Care*, OECD Publishing, Paris, http://dx.doi.org/10.1787/9789264276116-3-en. [10]

OECD (2017), *Starting Strong V: Transitions from Early Childhood Education and Care to Primary Education*, Starting Strong, OECD Publishing, Paris, https://dx.doi.org/10.1787/9789264276253-en. [6]

OECD (2016), *PISA 2015 Results (Volume II): Policies and Practices for Successful Schools*, PISA, OECD Publishing, Paris, http://dx.doi.org/10.1787/9789264267510-en.   [16]

OECD (2015), *Starting Strong IV: Monitoring Quality in Early Childhood Education and Care*, Starting Strong, OECD Publishing, Paris, http://dx.doi.org/10.1787/9789264233515-en.   [5]

OECD (2014), *New Insights from TALIS 2013: Teaching and Learning in Primary and Upper Secondary Education*, TALIS, OECD Publishing, Paris, https://dx.doi.org/10.1787/9789264226319-en.   [11]

OECD (2011), *Starting strong III: A Quality Toolbox for Early Childhood Education and Care*, OECD Publishing, Paris, http://dx.doi.org/10.1787/9789264123564-en.   [4]

OECD (2006), *Starting Strong II: Early Childhood Education and Care*, Starting Strong, OECD Publishing, Paris, http://dx.doi.org/10.1787/9789264035461-en.   [3]

OECD (2001), *Starting Strong: Early Childhood Education and Care*, Starting Strong, OECD Publishing, Paris, http://dx.doi.org/10.1787/9789264192829-en.   [2]

Petitclerc, A. et al. (2017), "Who uses early childhood education and care services? Comparing socioeconomic selection across five western policy contexts", *International Journal of Child Care and Education Policy*, Vol. 11/1, http://dx.doi.org/10.1186/s40723-017-0028-8.   [25]

Reid, J. and D. Ready (2013), "High-Quality Preschool: The Socioeconomic Composition of Preschool Classrooms and Children's Learning", *Early Education & Development*, Vol. 24/8, pp. 1082-1111, http://dx.doi.org/10.1080/10409289.2012.757519.   [36]

Ribeiro, L. and H. Zachrisson (2017), "Peer Effects on Aggressive Behavior in Norwegian Child Care Centers", *Child Development*, http://dx.doi.org/10.1111/cdev.12953.   [34]

Ribeiro, L., H. Zachrisson and E. Dearing (2017), "Peer effects on the development of language skills in Norwegian childcare centers", *Early Childhood Research Quarterly*, Vol. 41, pp. 1-12, http://dx.doi.org/10.1016/j.ecresq.2017.05.003.   [35]

Sammons, P. et al. (2008), *Children's Cognitive Attainment and Progress in English Primary Schools During Key Stage 2: Investigating the potential continuing influences of pre-school education*, VS Verlag für Sozialwissenschaften, http://dx.doi.org/10.1007/978-3-531-91452-7_12.   [12]

Schweinhart, L. and D. Weikart (1997), "The high/scope preschool curriculum comparison study through age 23", *Early Childhood Research Quarterly*, Vol. 12/2, pp. 117-143, http://dx.doi.org/10.1016/s0885-2006(97)90009-0.   [19]

Sibley, E. et al. (2015), "Do increased availability and reduced cost of early childhood care and education narrow social inequality gaps in utilization? Evidence from Norway", *International Journal of Child Care and Education Policy*, Vol. 9/1, http://dx.doi.org/10.1007/s40723-014-0004-5.   [27]

Sim, M. et al. (2018), *Teaching, Pedagogy and Practice in Early Years Childcare: An Evidence Review*, Early Intervention Foundation.   [29]

Sylva, K. et al. (2004), *The Effective Provision of Pre-school Education (EPPE) project: Final Report - A longitudinal study funded by the DfES 1997-2004*, Institute of Education, University of London/ Department for Education and Skills/ Sure Start, London.   [13]

Yoshikawa, H. and S. Kabay (2015), *The Evidence Base on Early Childhood Care and Education in Global Contexts*, UNESCO, Paris, http://unesdoc.unesco.org/images/0023/002324/232456e.pdf.   [9]

Zachrisson, H. and E. Dearing (2014), "Family Income Dynamics, Early Childhood Education and Care, and Early Child Behavior Problems in Norway", *Child Development*, Vol. 86/2, pp. 425-440, http://dx.doi.org/10.1111/cdev.12306.   [24]

Zachrisson, H., H. Janson and A. Nærde (2013), "Predicting early center care utilization in a context of universal access", *Early Childhood Research Quarterly*, Vol. 28/1, pp. 74-82, http://dx.doi.org/10.1016/j.ecresq.2012.06.004.   [28]

POLICIES FOR EARLY LEARNING: WORK ORGANISATION AND STAFF QUALIFICATIONS

This chapter examines two aspects of quality as the term relates to early childhood education and care: structural characteristics and process quality. Structural characteristics refer to the work organisation, including working hours, staff salaries and the ratio of children to staff, and staff qualifications in a given programme. Process quality is defined as children's interactions with staff and with the other children in their group. The chapter discusses the research showing how the interplay of these various components can affect the quality of early childhood education and care.

A growing body of research suggests that the magnitude of the benefits of early education and care for children depends on the quality of the services provided. Low-quality programmes have been associated with no benefits or even with detrimental effects on children's development and learning (Britto, Yoshikawa and Boller, 2011[1]; Howes et al., 2008[2]). With mounting pressure to provide more affordable places in early childhood education and care programmes, in a sector that is often highly decentralised, it can be particularly daunting to improve quality – particularly when public budgets are being tightened. That makes it even more important to have a clear understanding of the dimensions of quality that matter most for child development.

DIMENSIONS OF "QUALITY" IN EARLY CHILDHOOD EDUCATION AND CARE

The definitions of quality in early childhood education and care often distinguish between structural characteristics and process quality (OECD, 2018[3]).

Structural characteristics are more distal indicators of the quality of early childhood education and care. They refer to the infrastructure, i.e. the available physical, human and material resources. Structural characteristics tend to be aspects of the early childhood education and care system that are easier to regulate, such as child-staff ratio, group size and staff training/ education. These characteristics can often be measured through surveys or interviews at the classroom, setting or system level.

Process quality concerns the more proximal aspects of children's daily experience. It includes the social, emotional, physical and instructional aspects of children's interactions with staff members and other children (peer interactions) while involved in play, more structured activities or routines. Staff-child interactions include: the emotional climate, including physical and emotional care and support; instructional quality or pedagogical practices, including the strategies and activities staff use to engage children in learning and development, and how they scaffold children's learning; and the organisation of group routines and the management of children's behaviour.

Additional aspects of process quality include the quality of children's interactions with the space and materials available (Hamre et al., 2014[4]; Mashburn et al., 2008[5]; Slot et al., 2017[6]; Slot, 2017[7]). Interactions among children, among staff and with parents are also important. Children with involved parents tend to do better in reading and numeracy, have positive social and emotional social skills, and be more motivated to learn (OECD, 2017[8]). In addition, supportive relationships that generate healthy attachments positively affect children's understanding and regulation of emotions, their feelings of security and their taste for exploration and learning (OECD, 2015[9]).

The Programme for International Student Assessment (PISA) and many other studies show that children whose parents engage in certain activities, such as reading, writing words, telling stories and singing songs, not only tend to acquire better reading and numeracy skills, but are also more motivated to learn (Scottish Government, 2016[10]; OECD, 2011[11]; Sylva, Siraj-Blatchford and Taggart, 2003[12]; van Voorhis et al., 2013[13]). Differences in developmental outcomes related to gender and socio-economic status are observed early in life, before children start primary school (Bradbury et al., 2011[14]; Feinstein, 2003[15]; Sylva et al., 2004[16]). The role of parents, early childhood education and care staff, and school teachers in identifying children's individual need for support is thus vital.

Box 2.1. **Starting Strong: Improving the impact of early childhood education and care**

The benefits of early childhood education and care to children – and to society – depend greatly on the quality of those programmes. Traditionally, policies have focused on investments in structural quality, such as staff-child ratios, group size and staff qualifications. But research shows that the quality of early childhood environments is just as important for children's development, learning and well-being. Policy makers face complex decisions in investing in affordable high-quality programmes. With limited budgets, is it more important to raise the qualifications of staff or reduce group size? How can countries and jurisdictions address quality issues and access issues at the same time? To ensure that policy makers are informed of the evidence base, the OECD is conducting a Policy Review on Quality beyond Regulations in Early Childhood Education and Care and the Starting Strong Teaching and Learning International Survey.

Policy Review on Quality beyond Regulations in Early Childhood Education and Care (Starting Strong VI)

The Quality beyond Regulations review aims to help countries better understand the different quality dimensions of early childhood education and care programmes, focusing on policy interventions that enhance process quality and that can ensure better child development, learning and well-being. It will give countries the opportunity to participate in the first international comparative review of process quality and engage in peer-learning activities. It will also help countries monitor, collect and interpret system-, staff- and child-level data on the quality of early childhood education and care.

...

Going beyond regulations means focusing on the multiple facets of process quality that determine how these programmes shape children's development, i.e. how children relate to their peers, the staff, parents, communities, and the space and materials available to them. The Quality beyond Regulations project seeks to identify how policy levers, such as curriculum, pedagogy and workforce development, can improve the quality of these interactions.

Next milestones: County survey and background reports on policies and practices to foster process quality (2019); multidimensional matrix/framework on quality (2020); international synthesis report Starting Strong VI (2021).

Starting Strong Teaching and Learning International Survey

The first-ever international early childhood education and care staff survey builds on the established OECD Teaching and Learning International Survey (TALIS) to provide early childhood staff and centre leaders with an opportunity to share insights on their professional development; pedagogical beliefs and practices; and working conditions, as well as various other leadership, management and workplace issues.

The data on the quality of learning and well-being environments in early childhood settings, collected in nine OECD countries, will benefit policy makers in two ways: they will highlight differences between reported early childhood professional and pedagogical practices within and across countries and systems; and they will enrich the analysis of the impact of early childhood education and care policies on children's learning and well-being environments. For instance, the project will investigate how the structural characteristics of these settings are linked to staff members' beliefs, practices and interactions with colleagues and children.

Next milestones: International database and report (Vol. I) on ensuring quality learning and well-being environments in early childhood education and care centres (2019); thematic report on staff and centres for children under the age of three; report (Vol. II) on building a high-quality early childhood education and care workforce (2020).

WORK ORGANISATION IN EARLY CHILDHOOD EDUCATION

In order to attract the most suitable candidates to the early childhood education and care workforce, countries need not only to offer adequate pay but also provide an environment where leaders and other staff are given the autonomy, and have the time and space to work as professionals. In this respect, statutory working hours and the child-to-staff ratio are two important system-level indicators to assess the quality of the early childhood centre environment.

Workload refers to the number of working hours, indicating the extent to which staff schedules are compatible with family life and the physical demands of the job. Large groups, low staff-child ratios and a heavy workload are potential stressors for staff. Some research findings show the effects of workload on the quality of early childhood education and care, indicating that practitioners with a heavy workload perform less well than colleagues with lighter schedules (de Schipper, Riksen-Walraven and Geurts, 2007[17]).

Research has shown that staff members' job satisfaction and retention – and therefore the quality of early childhood education and care – can be improved by: reducing both child-staff ratios and group size; providing competitive wages and other benefits; setting reasonable schedules/workloads; reducing staff turnover; providing a good physical environment; and employing a competent and supportive centre manager.

Common challenges that countries face in establishing a high-quality workforce include: raising the qualifications of staff; recruiting, retaining and diversifying a qualified workforce; continuously up-dating the skills of the workforce; and ensuring the quality of the workforce in the private sector. Various strategies have been undertaken to address these challenges using legal instruments, institutional rearrangements, financial incentives and data to inform policy makers and the public. The following sections examine some of these factors in greater detail. Most of the data in this chapter are taken from the OECD reports *Starting Strong III: A Quality Toolbox for Early Childhood Education and Care* (OECD, 2011[11]), *Starting Strong 2017: Key OECD Indicators on Early Childhood Education and Care* (OECD, 2017[18]) and *Education at a Glance 2018* (OECD, 2018[19]).

Working hours

Although statutory working hours and contact hours with children only partly determine teachers' actual workload, they do offer valuable insights into the demands placed on teachers in different countries. Contact hours with children and the extent of non-teaching duties may also affect the attractiveness of the profession.

At the pre-primary level of education, countries vary considerably in the number of contact hours with children per year required of the average early childhood education and care teacher working in a public setting. Required contact time with children at this level in public programmes varies more across countries than it does at any other level of education. The

number of teaching days per year ranges from 157 in the Flemish Community of Belgium to more than 220 in Germany and Iceland. Annual contact time of teachers with children ranges from less than 600 hours per year in Korea and Mexico to more than 1 600 hours in Germany and Iceland. On average across OECD countries, teachers at this level of education are required to be in contact with children 1 029 hours per year, spread over 40 weeks or 196 days of teaching (Figure 2.1).

Translated into hours per day, teachers are required to be in contact with children between 4 and 6 hours a day in 17 out of 28 countries with available data. The main exceptions are Germany, Iceland and Latvia, where teachers are in contact with children more than 6.5 hours per day in pre-primary education, and Korea and Mexico, where they are in contact with children less than 4 hours per day. There is no set rule on how contact time is distributed throughout the year across OECD countries. In Poland, for example, pre-primary teachers must teach 1 085 hours per year, about 56 hours more than the OECD average. However, those contact hours with children are spread over 21 more days of instruction than the OECD average. As a result, pre-primary teachers in Poland teach an average of 5 hours per day, which is around the same number of hours per day as the OECD average (Figure 2.1).

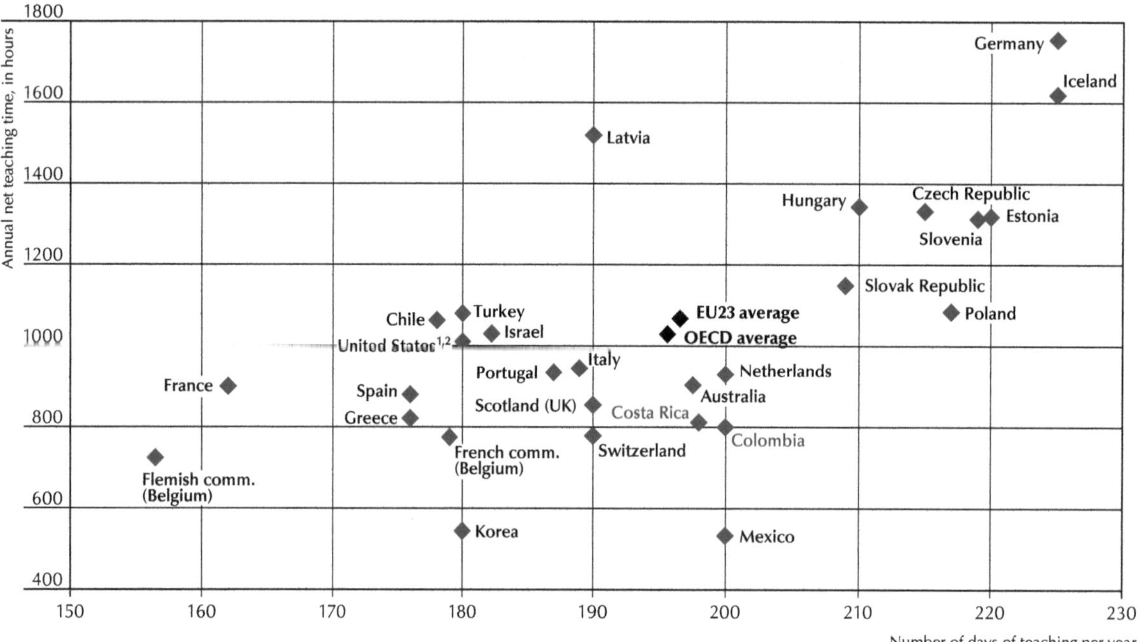

Figure 2.1

Organisation of annual teachers' contact time with children in pre-primary public institutions (2017)

1. Actual teaching time.
2. Year of reference 2016.
Source: OECD (2018), *Education at a Glance 2018: OECD Indicators*, OECD Publishing, Paris, https://dx.doi.org/10.1787/eag-2018-en.

Child-to-staff ratios

In addition to working hours, workload and salary, a low child-to-staff ratio affects working conditions, which, in turn, have an impact on job satisfaction and retention, and through these, contributes to the quality of early childhood education and care services (Clarke-Stewart et al., 2002[20]; Burchinal et al., 2002[21]; Huntsman, 2008[22]). Smaller ratios are often seen as beneficial because they allow staff to focus more on the needs of individual pupils and reduce the amount of class time needed to deal with disruptions. Staff effectiveness is also affected by the size of the groups: smaller groups are beneficial for enhancing process quality (de Schipper, Riksen-Walraven and Geurts, 2007[17]; Burchinal et al., 2002[21]; Huntsman, 2008[22]).

The child-staff ratio is one of the key variables that policy makers can use to control spending on education. It is therefore an important indicator of the resources invested in early childhood education and care, and of the quality of these services. At the pre-primary level, there are 14 children for every teacher, on average across OECD countries. This number varies widely across countries with available data, ranging from more than 20 children per teacher in Brazil, Chile, Colombia, France, Mexico and South Africa to fewer than 10 children for every teacher in Iceland and Slovenia.

However, some countries make extensive use of teaching assistants at the pre-primary level. Ten OECD countries (and one partner country) reported smaller child-to-staff ratios than child-to-teacher ratios. Few of these countries employ large

numbers of teaching assistants. As a result, the child-to-staff ratios are substantially lower than child-to-teacher ratios (three children or fewer) only in Austria, Brazil, Chile, France, Lithuania and Norway (Figure 2.2).

Wide variations are also observed between early childhood development programmes (ISCED 01) and pre-primary education (ISCED 02), although a common pattern has emerged. In most countries with available data for both programmes, the ratios of children to contact staff (and of children to teacher) are smaller in early childhood development programmes (ISCED 01) than in pre-primary education (ISCED 02). On average across OECD countries, there are 14 children for each teacher working in pre-primary education, while the ratio is only 8 children per teacher in early childhood development programmes. When other staff are taken into account, the ratio of children to contact staff in early childhood development programmes is equal to or exceeds 7 only in Brazil, Costa Rica, Hungary and Lithuania.

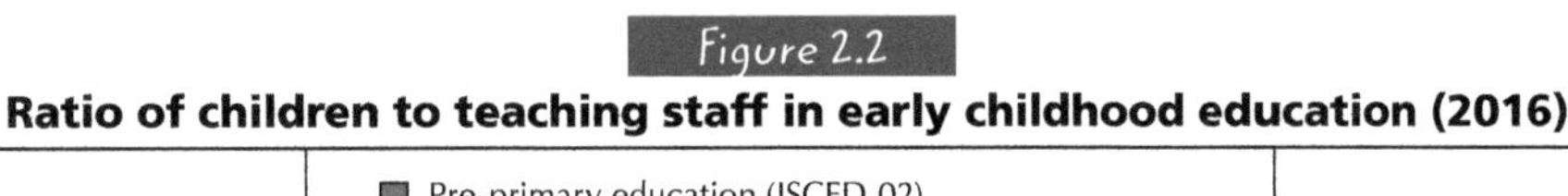

Figure 2.2
Ratio of children to teaching staff in early childhood education (2016)

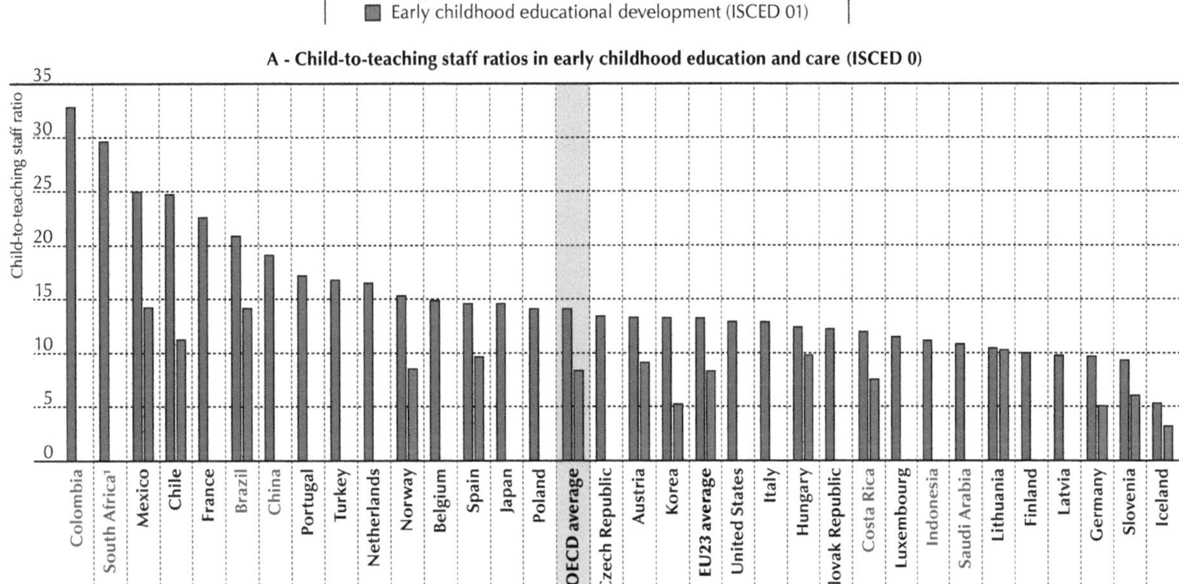

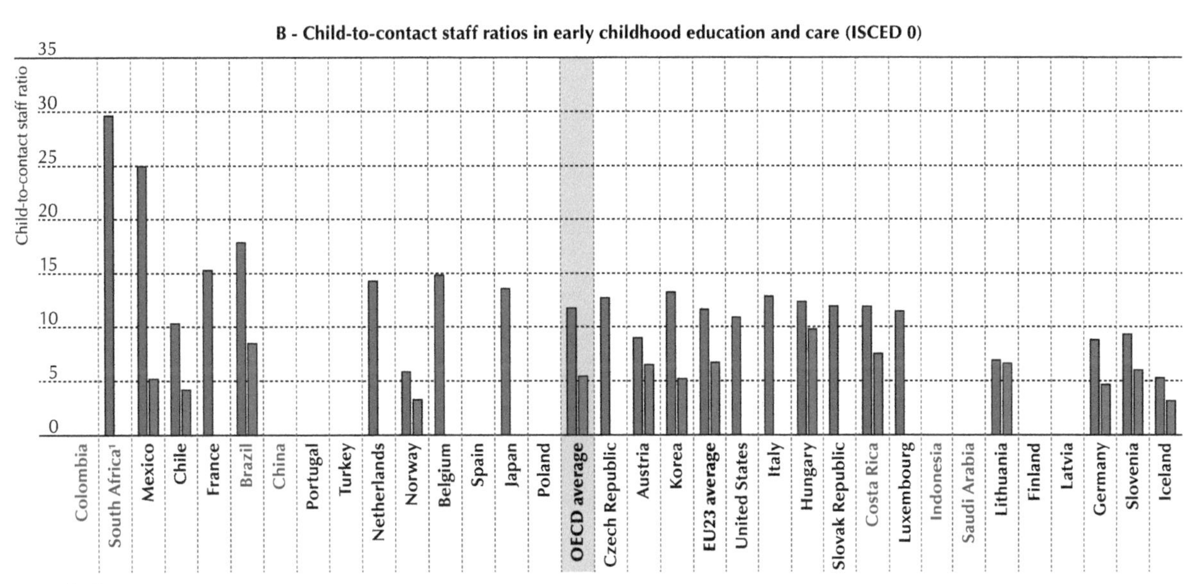

1. Year of reference 2015.
Countries are ranked in descending order of children-to-teacher ratios in pre-primary education.
Source: OECD (2018), *Education at a Glance 2018: OECD Indicators*, OECD Publishing, Paris, https://dx.doi.org/10.1787/eag-2018-en.

Staff salaries

Salaries affect job satisfaction and teachers' effectiveness (Huntsman, 2008[22]; Moon and Burbank, 2004[23]; Murnane et al., 1990[24]). There is some evidence that low salaries influence staff behaviour towards children and increase turnover rates (Huntsman, 2008[22]). Furthermore, low salaries may deter skilled professionals from choosing to work in early childhood education and care (Manlove and Guzell, 1997[25]).

Positive associations are found between salaries, a centre's organisational climate, and staff-child interactions, but the number of studies that have included these aspects is somewhat limited. Preliminary evidence suggests when staff are better paid and collaborate more with each other, centres catering to children from 3 to 6 years, and those catering to children under the age of 3 provided higher-quality staff-child interactions.

However, in early childhood education and care, there are large variations across countries in teachers' salaries, both in absolute terms and relative to national income. For instance, the annual statutory salary of pre-primary school teachers with 15 years of experience (before taxes and converted into USD using purchasing power parity) ranges from less than USD 15 000 in Lithuania and the Slovak Republic, to more than USD 50 000 in Australia, the Flemish Community of Belgium, Korea, the Netherlands and the United States, and exceeds USD 100 000 in Luxembourg (Figure 2.3).

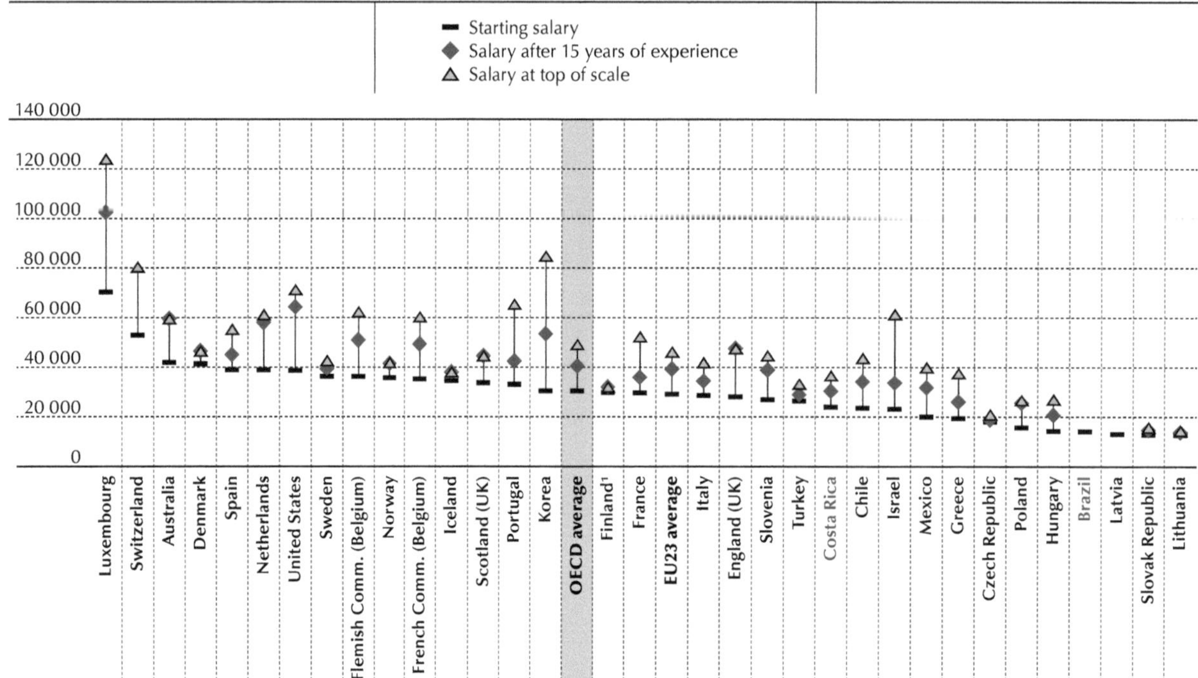

Figure 2.3

Annual statutory teachers' salaries in pre-primary education (2017)

Based on the most prevalent qualifications in public institutions, in equivalent USD converted using PPPs for private consumption.

1. Data on pre-primary teachers includes the salary of kindergarten teachers who are the majority.
Note: Statutory salaries, based on pay scales, are only one component of teachers' total compensation. Education systems also offer additional payments to teachers, such as allowances, bonuses or other rewards.
Countries are ranked in descending order of starting salaries for pre-primary teachers.
Source: OECD (2018), *Education at a Glance 2018: OECD Indicators*, Indicator D3, Table D3.1a., https://doi.org/10.1787/19991487.

Pre-primary systems differ not only in how much they pay teachers, but in the structure of their pay scale. On average, salaries increase by 63% from starting pay to the top of the salary scale, but there are wide variations across countries. For instance, some countries, such as the Czech Republic, Denmark, Finland, Iceland, Lithuania, Norway and Sweden, offer small salary increases over a teacher's career. Others, such as Israel, Korea and Mexico, offer greater rewards to more experienced teachers, who salaries can more than double between starting pay and the salary at the top of the scale (Figure 2.3).

STAFF QUALIFICATIONS

Although research emphasises the importance of adequate initial education and continuous professional development opportunities for staff, countries differ widely in the qualifications they demand of their early childhood education and

care practitioners. Opportunities to participate in professional development and in-service training also vary greatly across countries, and between education and child care in split systems. The qualification requirements vary from no formal education at all to a specialised bachelor's or even master's degree; professional development and training ranges from being compulsory to optional, sometimes with no additional funding for training (OECD, 2006[26]).

In 16 out of 22 countries with available data in 2017, more than three in four pre-primary teachers had completed a bachelor's degree or equivalent (ISCED level 6). In the Czech Republic, 77% of pre-primary teachers had not completed ISCED 6; this is by far the largest share among OECD countries with available data. The other countries where at least one in four teachers had not attained that level of education are Brazil, Estonia, Finland, Slovenia and Sweden. By contrast, in Poland and Portugal, 88% of pre-primary teachers had completed at least a master's degree or a doctoral or equivalent degree (ISCED 7 or 8). In the United States, 51% of pre-primary teachers had attained this level of education.

These data show that the duration of initial teacher training for pre-primary teachers ranges widely across OECD countries (OECD, 2018[19]).

The qualifications required indicate what knowledge and skills are recognised as important for working with young children. The competencies identified as particularly important for providing high-quality services are:

- good understanding of child development and learning

- ability to develop children's perspectives

- ability to praise, comfort, question and be responsive to children

- leadership skills, problem solving and development of targeted lesson plans

- good vocabulary and ability to elicit children's ideas.

Staff with higher qualifications can create a more stimulating environment and use more appropriate pedagogical practices, which boost children's well-being and learning outcomes (Litjens and Taguma, 2010[27]; Early et al., 2007[28]; Fontaine et al., 2006[29]; Phillipsen et al., 1997[30]). It is not the qualification per se that has an impact on child outcomes but the ability of better-qualified staff members to create a high-quality pedagogic environment that makes the difference (Elliott, 2006[31]; Sheridan et al., 2009[32]). There is strong evidence that enriching and stimulating environments and high-quality pedagogy are fostered by better-qualified staff; and better-quality pedagogy leads to better learning outcomes (Litjens and Taguma, 2010[27]). Key indicators of the quality of staff are the way staff involve children and stimulate interaction with and among children, and staff members' scaffolding strategies, such as guiding, modelling and questioning. Having more specialised staff is associated with stable, sensitive and stimulating interactions (Shonkoff and Phillips, 2000[33]). Other indicators include staff members' content (curriculum) knowledge and their ability to create a multi-disciplinary learning environment.

However, not all studies support the general conclusion that higher qualifications among the staff of early childhood education and care programmes lead to better pedagogical quality and, therefore, to better child outcomes. Early et al. emphasise that teacher quality is a complex issue (Early et al., 2007[28]). There is no simple relationship between the level of education of staff and classroom quality or learning outcomes. Early et al. studied the relationship between child outcomes and staff qualifications and found no, or contradictory, associations between the two.

Improving the effectiveness of early childhood education will likely require a broad range of professional development activities and support for the staff's interactions with children. One way to improve pedagogical practices used in these programmes is to enhance the staff's competence to communicate and interact with children in a shared and sustainable manner (Sheridan et al., 2009[32]). Research also finds that it is not necessary for all staff to have attained high levels of education. Highly qualified staff can have a positive influence on those who work with them but do not have the same high qualifications. The Effective Provision of Pre-School Education study finds that the observed behaviour of lower-qualified staff turns out to be positively influenced when these staff members work alongside highly trained colleagues (Sammons, 2010[34]).

Most countries have a wide range of qualifications for staff working in the early childhood education and care sector. Kindergarten/preschool teachers generally have higher initial education requirements than care centre staff or family care staff; some countries have a single qualification for all workers. Initial education for kindergarten/preschool teachers is often integrated with that of primary school teachers to ensure a smooth transition for children. More professional development opportunities are available for kindergarten/preschool staff than for care centre staff, with only limited

opportunities for family childcare staff. Professional development tends to focus on: pedagogies and instructional practices; curriculum implementation; language and subject matter; monitoring and assessment; and communication and management (OECD, 2011[11]).

However, no matter how high the quality of pre-service training, initial training cannot be expected to prepare teachers for all the challenges they will face throughout their careers. Given the changes in student demographics, the length of most teachers' careers, and the need to update knowledge and competencies, initial teacher education must be viewed as only the starting point for teachers' ongoing development. Recent research also shows that in pre-primary education, the effects of specialised in-service training on process quality are larger than those of pre-service training, particularly when it comes to collaborative work, support for play, and support for early literacy, mathematics and science (Assel et al., 2006[35]; de Haan et al., 2013[36]).

In-service (ongoing) education and training can be conducted "on the job" or provided by an external source, such as a training institute or college. It can be provided through, for instance, staff meetings, workshops, conferences, subject training, field-based consultation training, supervised practices and mentoring. The key to effective professional development is identifying the right training strategies to help early childhood education and care practitioners stay up-to-date on scientifically based methods and curriculum subject knowledge so as to be able to apply this knowledge in their work (Litjens and Taguma, 2010[27]). This type of training should continue over a longer period of time, and staff should have long-term or regular opportunities for training (Sheridan, 2001[37]). Only when learning experiences are targeted to the needs of staff can professional development have favourable outcomes (Mitchell and Cubey, 2003[38]).

Field-based consultation can also be effective, as it provides early childhood education and care staff with the possibility to receive feedback on their practices. Practitioners who do not hold a degree, but who attend relevant professional workshops are found to provide higher-quality care than colleagues who do not attend such workshops (Burchinal et al., 2002[21]). However, in general, there is little clarity about what forms of professional development are most effective. One reason is that staff have different needs and training backgrounds. Effective training should address these differences (Elliott, 2006[31]).

Despite the evidence of the benefits of having well-trained early education and care staff, governments often fear the financial consequences of raising staff qualifications. Higher qualifications may be followed by demands for higher wages, which, in turn, contribute significantly to the cost of services. Although the evidence is strong that improved training and qualifications raise the quality of early childhood education and care services, governments often choose not to invest in raising qualifications or staff training (OECD, 2006[26]). This might affect the quality of early childhood education and care, and with this, child development outcomes, since staff are not being optimally trained to stimulate early learning and development.

USING WORK ORGANISATION AND STAFF QUALIFICATIONS AS "QUALITY DRIVERS"

Policy makers face complex decisions on spending for early childhood education and care. They need to consider trade-offs between structural investments and investments that improve the quality of the interactions between staff and children. In order to make informed decisions, policy makers need to consult the evidence base so that they can examine how certain policy options apply to their context or jurisdiction. The following sections summarise research findings concerning how work organisation and staff qualifications affect structural and process quality. The information is taken from the OECD report, *Engaging Young Children*, prepared as part of the Quality beyond Regulations project (OECD, 2018[3]).

The quality of child-staff interactions

The meta-analysis conducted for the Quality beyond Regulations project indicate a consistent positive association between the quality of staff-child interactions and children's literacy and numeracy learning (Figure 2.4) (von Suchodoletz et al., 2017[39]). This association is observed when considering an overall staff-child interactions index (Panel A), and also a combined score of staff emotional, instructional and organisational interactions with the children (Panel B).

Conversely, no associations were found between the quality of staff-child interactions and children's behavioural/social skills using the overall staff-child interactions index (von Suchodoletz et al., 2017[39]).

Figure 2.4

More positive staff-child interactions are associated with higher levels of child emerging academic skills

Global score of staff-child interactions

	Effect size	Confidence interval	
		Low	High
US - Burchinal et al. (2014)	0.230	0.157	0.300
US - Vandell et al. (2010)	0.230	0.169	0.289
US - McGinty et al. (2012)	0.150	0.050	0.247
Germany - Anders et al. (2012)	0.140	0.056	0.222
Germany - Richter et al. (2016)	0.125	-0.003	0.249
US - Buckrop et al. (2016)	0.120	0.057	0.182
US - Chang et al. (2007)	0.110	0.004	0.213
Portugal - Abreu-Lima (2013)	0.090	-0.044	0.221
US - Coley et al. (2016)	-0.020	-0.050	0.010
US - Howes et al. (2008)	-0.030	-0.071	0.011
Strict Combined Result	0.052	0.033	0.070
Combined Result	0.113	0.041	0.183

Combined score of emotional, instructional and organisational staff-child interactions

	Effect size	Confidence interval	
		Low	High
US - Burchinal et al. (2014)	0.230	0.157	0.300
US - Vandell et al. (2010)	0.230	0.169	0.289
US - McGinty et al. (2012)	0.150	0.050	0.247
US - Burchinal et al. (2010)	0.082	0.023	0.139
US - Buckrop et al. (2016)	0.080	0.017	0.143
US - Burchinal et al. (2011)	0.070	-0.036	0.174
US - Chang et al. (2007)	0.050	-0.056	0.155
US - Guo et al. (2010)	0.048	-0.060	0.156
US - Howes et al. (2008)	0.018	-0.023	0.059
Australia - Niklas et al. (2016)	0.018	-0.088	0.123
US - Burchinal et al. (2014)	-0.082	-0.149	-0.015
Strict Combined Result	0.031	0.007	0.055

Note: Blue colouring shows a positive association between staff-child interactions and children's emerging academic skills; grey colouring shows a negative association. The darker colouring indicates that the interaction is positive or negative even after accounting for the confidence interval. The lower and upper limits show the 95% confidence interval for each estimated effect.
Source: von Suchodoletz, A. et al. (2017), *"Associations among quality indicators in early childhood education and care (ECEC) and relations with child development and learning: A meta-analysis"*, internal document, OECD, Paris.

Exposure to developmental and educational activities

The meta-analysis conducted for the Quality beyond Regulations project also examined the association between staff implementing developmental and educational activities, a process-quality indicator of the workforce, and children's emerging academic skills The results show that children have slightly higher levels of emerging literacy and numeracy skills, and better behavioural and social skills, in early childhood education and care centres where staff provide higher quality or more exposure to developmental and educational activities (OECD, 2018[3]).

Child-staff ratios

Low child-staff ratios were found to enhance positive staff-child relationships across all types of settings, and early childhood education and care age groups. Multiple studies of individual countries, including China, Portugal and the United States, and a meta-analysis of 17 studies from Europe and North America suggest that a smaller number of children per staff member tends to be associated with higher process quality for centres catering to children aged 3 to 5. While the association was not found everywhere, there is no evidence of any negative effects.

Figure 2.5

Greater exposure to developmental and educational activities is associated with higher levels of children's skills

Children's emerging academic skills

	Effect size	Confidence interval	
		Low	High
Germany - Anders et al. (2012)	0.130	0.045	0.213
US - McGinty et al. (2012)	0.035	-0.066	0.135
US - Howes et al. (2008)	0.020	-0.021	0.061
US - Coley et al. (2016)	0.016	-0.014	0.046
Portugal - Abreu-Lima (2013)	0.000	-0.134	0.134
Chile - Strasser et al. (2009)	-0.020	-0.194	0.155
Strict Combined Result	0.025	0.003	0.047
Combined Result	0.030	-0.001	0.061

Combined score of child behaviour and social skills

	Effect size	Confidence interval	
		Low	High
Germany - Anders et al. (2012)	0.110	0.025	0.193
Portugal - Abreu-Lima (2013)	0.090	-0.044	0.221
US - Coley et al. (2016)	0.023	-0.007	0.053
Strict Combined Result	0.035	0.007	0.063

Note: Blue colouring shows a positive association between exposure to developmental and educational activities and children's skills; grey colouring shows a negative association. The darker colouring indicates that the interaction is positive or negative even after accounting for the confidence interval. The lower and upper limits show the 95% confidence interval for each estimated effect.
Source: von Suchodoletz, A. et al. (2017), *"Associations among quality indicators in early childhood education and care (ECEC) and relations with child development and learning: A meta-analysis"*, internal document, OECD, Paris.

Lower child-staff ratios were also associated with more positive interactions for children aged zero to 3 in the Flemish Community of Belgium, the Netherlands, Portugal and the United States. These findings were more conclusive for centre-based settings than for family childcare, where groups are usually much smaller (OECD, 2018[3]).

Group size

Some supporting evidence suggests that smaller groups improve staff-child interactions in settings for younger children. In looking at services for children aged 0 to 2, both group size and staff-child ratios were found to affect the quality of staff-child interactions, even though a few studies did not find associations. These findings were more conclusive for centre-based settings than for family daycare, where groups are usually much smaller. For the older age group, evidence can be found in both directions, which does not indicate that having smaller groups presents a clear benefit. No research on potential direct associations of group size with child development was available for this report (Barros et al., 2016[40]; Hulpia et al., 2016[41]; OECD, 2018[3]).

Relationships between quality indicators

Despite some evidence from the United States showing an association between child-staff ratios and children's pre-reading scores in preschool (Bigras, Lemay and Tremblay, 2012[42]; Cardon et al., 2008[43]; Howes, 1997[44]), there seems no solid evidence of direct links to child development and learning across age groups. Tentative results suggest that those structures for processing relationships could be non-linear, i.e. that reducing the size of a small group may have effects that are different from reducing the size of a large group (Bowne et al., 2017[45]).

A review of the literature indicated a mixed pattern of associations across age groups, and there was no relationship between low child-staff ratios and emerging academic skills, i.e. early literacy and numeracy (OECD, 2018[3]). There is, however, some preliminary evidence of indirect paths from ratios through staff-child interactions to children's development, but the associations are weak and need further confirmation (NICHD Early Child Care Research Network, 2002[46]).

In a couple of studies, the relationship between organisational climate and quality has been found to be even stronger than other classroom characteristics, such as the child-staff ratio (Biersteker et al., 2016[47]; Dennis and O'Connor, 2013[48]),

and staff characteristics, including qualifications and work experience (Biersteker et al., 2016[47]). However, organisational climate itself is also associated with other centre characteristics (Ho, Lee and Teng, 2016[49]).

Pre-service training

Overall, higher pre-service qualifications were found to be related to better staff-child interactions in Germany, Denmark, Portugal and the United States. Across the age groups in early childhood education and care, in home- and in centre-based settings, more pre-service training is associated with higher levels of staff's emotional, instructional and organisational interactions, especially if the training includes content on early childhood education and care. Pre-service training specifically enhances emotionally supportive interactions, and more educational and developmental interactions (OECD, 2018[3]).

The evidence has also shown a strong association between pre-service qualifications and staff-child interactions for children aged 0 to 2 in Quebec, the Flemish Community of Belgium, the Netherlands, Portugal and the United States (Barros et al., 2016[40]; Bigras et al., 2010[50]; Castle et al., 2016[51]; Hulpia et al., 2016[41]; King et al., 2016[52]; Slot et al., 2015[53]; Thomason and La Paro, 2009[54]; Vogel et al., 2015[55]; Vogel et al., 2015[56]).

However, evidence shows a weak or unclear direct link between pre-service qualifications and the learning and development of 3-5 year-old children (von Suchodoletz et al., 2017[39]). Higher staff qualifications were not associated with emerging academic skills, or behavioural/social skills (Early et al., 2006[57]; Mashburn et al., 2008[5]).

Licensing family childcare

The limited available evidence on family childcare suggests that, for the youngest children, licensed providers with higher pre-service qualifications offer more diverse learning experiences and activities. In the United States and the Flemish Community of Belgium, they also demonstrate more active involvement and guidance in these activities than less-educated family childcare providers (Colwell et al., 2013[58]; Doherty et al., 2006[59]; Raikes, Raikes and Wilcox, 2005[60]; Schaack, Le and Setodji, 2017[61]) (Hulpia et al., 2016[41]; Vandenbroeck et al., 2018[62]).

However, there is no evidence for direct links between pre-service training of family childcare providers and child development.

In-service training

In a variety of countries, including China, Denmark, Portugal and the United States, in-service training (or professional development) was consistently and positively associated with staff interactions with children – in all settings and for all age groups examined (Fukkink and Lont, 2007[63]; Hamre et al., 2012[64]; Justice et al., 2008[65]; LoCassale-Crouch et al., 2011[66]; Slot et al., 2018[67]; Slot, Lerkkanen and Leseman, 2015[68]; Zaslow et al., 2010[69]), especially if the training included early childhood education and care content, for instance related to staff-child interactions (Siraj-Blatchford et al., 2005[70]; Zaslow et al., 2004[71]). Staff participating in in-service training have consistently been found to score higher on language and literacy-specific quality (Egert, 2015[72]); but evidence on the links to overall quality of early childhood education and care or staff-child interactions is mixed.

There is also consistent evidence, across all age groups, of a positive link between in-service training and children's development and learning, with the evidence particularly strong for children's language and literacy skills. The number of studies available involving children aged zero to 3 is more limited, but the pattern of results is largely consistent (OECD, 2018[3]).

Staff practices and engagement with children

Children in early childhood education and care centres with better staff-child interactions, or with staff who provide higher-quality or more exposure to developmental and educational activities were found to have higher levels of emerging literacy and numeracy skills, and better behavioural and social skills (von Suchodoletz et al., 2017[39]).

Positive associations were found between staff-child interactions, including higher-quality educational and developmental activities, with staff well-being, salaries and with centre organisational climate. Higher-quality organisational climate includes environments where staff believe that they enjoyed more autonomy and support for showing leadership, exchange their visions with colleagues more often, and report more opportunities for participating in decision-making related to the curriculum (OECD, 2018[3]).

While the number of studies that have included these structural aspects is somewhat limited, and research does not find evidence for effects of staff work experience (von Suchodoletz et al., 2017[39]), emerging evidence indicates that centres where staff reported greater well-being (including job satisfaction and lack of symptoms of depression), higher salaries and more team collaboration show better staff-child interactions across all age groups served (OECD, 2018[3]).

The early childhood education and care sector, especially that catering to the youngest children, suffers from staff shortages, high turnover and low status in many countries (Moon and Burbank, 2004[23]). When staff members regularly change, staff and children are less able to develop stable relationships and the frequency of nurturing, stimulating interactions is reduced (Canadian Council on Learning, 2006[73]). Political concerns about the quality of interactions thus support the case for improving working conditions – in the best interests of the children's learning experience and staff members' job satisfaction.

The research reviewed for the OECD report, *Engaging Young Children: Lessons from Research about Quality in Early Childhood Education and Care* (OECD, 2018[3]), did not examine links between working conditions and child development because research on those associations is neither extensive nor conclusive. There is a complex inter-relationship between child-staff ratios, staff qualifications, quality and types of settings. For instance, ratios relate to working conditions for staff and to learning and well-being environments for children. This makes it difficult to single out the effect of a particular characteristic of working conditions on process quality (Sammons, 2010[34]).

Sorting children

Targeting early childhood education and care to disadvantaged groups may seem a cost-effective way to ensure that services reach those who need them most, but concerns about quality need to be considered. The OECD study, *Engaging Young Children: Lessons from Research about Quality in Early Childhood Education and Care*, provides an overview of research suggesting that in playrooms or classrooms in Denmark, Germany and the United States, the quality of staff-child interactions was lower in those that had a high percentage of immigrant or bilingual children than in playrooms or classrooms with a more balanced or mixed-group composition (OECD, 2018[3]).

Classrooms with a high percentage of immigrant or bilingual children are also associated with lower scores in children's language and literacy skills. The evidence is more consistent for children aged 3 to 5 than for centres with younger children, which may be related to the targeted high-quality services for the youngest children in some countries. Negative associations between the percentage of immigrant or bilingual children and the quality of child-staff interactions were also observed in family childcare (OECD, 2018[3]).

Some preliminary evidence shows that lower levels of staff emotional support and classroom organisation may be the key to this relationship (Slot et al., 2018[67]). The associations between staff-child interactions and children's development and learning, however, do not seem to differ significantly for children from predominantly disadvantaged backgrounds compared to those in a mixed group of children.

Monitoring systems

In the United States, quality rating and improvement systems (QRIS) are found to be associated with higher levels of staff-child interactions in centres for all age groups (Jeon, Buettner and Hur, 2014[74]), while the linkage between QRIS and staff-child interactions in family childcare is less clear (Lahti et al., 2015[75]; Lipscomb et al., 2017[76]). Where evidence exists, there is an indication that positive feedback loops between monitoring systems and staff practices may be associated with gains in children's language development (OECD, 2015[9]). A key target of policy efforts might thus be to ensure that information on staff-child interactions in centres is collected not simply for the purpose of accountability, but used to inform improvements in quality.

Locating early childhood education and care centres within schools

In Finland, Portugal and the United States, the physical location of a preschool may also be related to process quality. Higher-quality staff-child relationships were observed in preschools located in schools, compared with preschools situated outside school grounds or in independent centres (Pianta et al., 2005[77]; Slot, 2017[7]; Slot, Lerkkanen and Leseman, 2015[68]). There is also evidence that staff working in classrooms located in schools are more educated, are paid more and show a stronger educational orientation than staff working in independent centres (Clifford et al., 2005[78]; Pianta et al., 2005[77]).

CONCLUSIONS

Policy makers need to make trade-offs between structural investments and investments that improve the quality of the interactions between early childhood education and care staff and children. However, the evidence base in this field is still limited and often narrow. Research on structural characteristics of early childhood education and care settings has often been dominated by a focus on the so-called "iron triangle" characteristics (i.e. child-staff ratio, group size and teachers' pre-service qualifications) (Slot, 2017[7]). To date, the vast majority of studies investigating associations between

structural characteristics and process quality focused on only one indicator of process quality: the quality of teacher-child interactions. The research has also largely overlooked many other aspects of process quality, such as child-to-child (peer) interactions. This chapter identifies a number of research findings concerning how work organisation and staff qualifications can be used to improve structural and process quality, namely:

- Lower child-staff ratios alone will not guarantee better child development; but they are associated with more positive staff-child relations across all age groups.

- Group size matters for staff-child interactions, but the association is stronger for interactions with the youngest children than with children aged 3 to 5.

- Relationships between quality indicators can be indirect, such as between ratios, group size, organisational climate, quality of staff-child interactions, and child development and learning.

- Pre-service training, when focusing on early childhood education and care content, is associated with better staff emotional, educational and developmental support for children, with a stronger relationship found when working with the youngest children. In contrast, the evidence on its association with learning outcomes is inconclusive.

- Licensing family childcare, when regulated with pre-service qualifications, can be a tool to ensure better interactions for children.

- In-service training that includes early childhood education and care-specific content is associated with better staff-child interactions, and better child development and learning outcomes, especially literacy skills, for all groups of children.

- Staff engagement with children in quality developmental activities may depend on team collaboration, and benefit from improved working conditions and well-being.

- Separate classrooms or playrooms for disadvantaged, immigrant or bilingual children are associated with a risk of inequity and poor quality of early childhood education and care.

- Monitoring systems, if they are used to inform quality improvements, are linked to greater support to children's development and learning in all early childhood education and care settings.

- Locating early childhood education and care centres within schools is associated with differences in staff members' relationships with children.

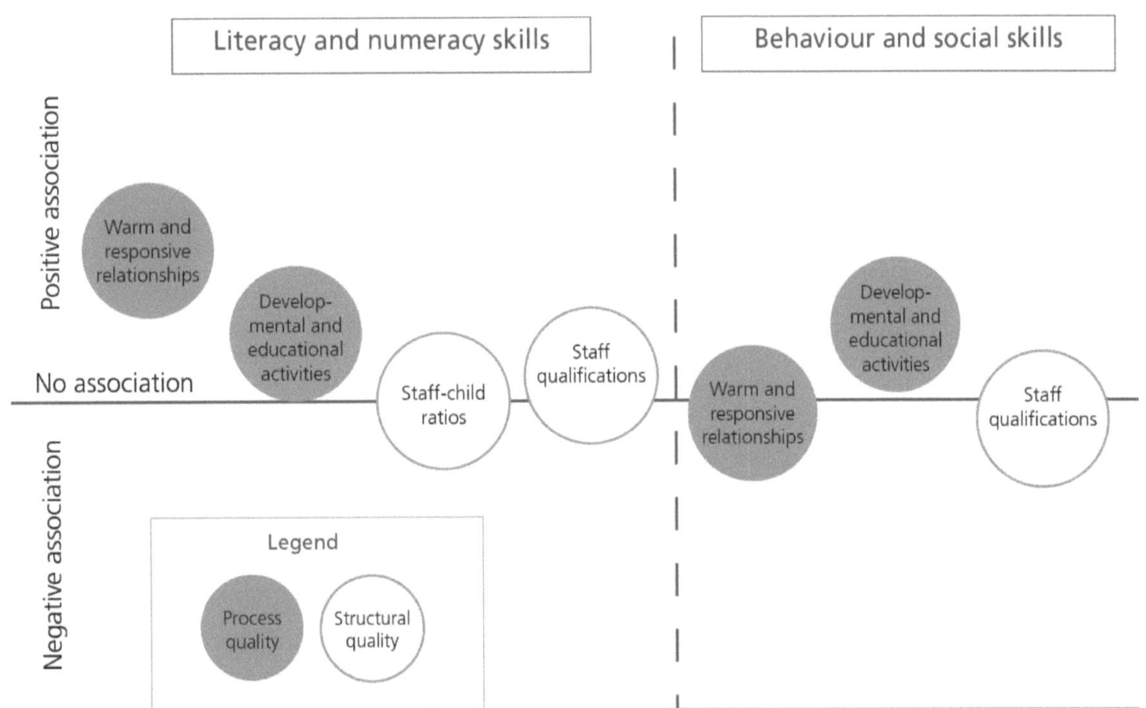

References

Assel, M. et al. (2006), "An evaluation of curriculum, setting, and mentoring on the performance of children enrolled in pre-kindergarten", *Reading and Writing*, Vol. 20/5, pp. 463-494, http://dx.doi.org/10.1007/s11145-006-9039-5.   [35]

Barros, S. et al. (2016), "Infant child care in Portugal: Associations with structural characteristics", *Early Childhood Research Quarterly*, Vol. 37/1, pp. 118-130, http://dx.doi.org/10.1016/j.ecresq.2016.05.003.   [40]

Biersteker, L. et al. (2016), "Center-based early childhood care and education program quality: A South- African study", *Early Childhood Research Quarterly*, Vol. 36, pp. 334-344, http://dx.doi.org/10.1016/j.ecresq.2016.01.004.   [47]

Bigras, N. et al. (2010), "A comparative study of structural and process quality in center-based and family-based child care services", *Child Youth Care Forum*, Vol. 39/3, pp. 129-150, http://dx.doi.org/10.1007/s10566-009-9088-4.   [50]

Bigras, N., L. Lemay and M. Tremblay (2012), *Petite enfance, services de garde éducatifs et développement des enfants : état des connaissances.*, Presses de l'Université du Québec, Montréal.   [42]

Bowne, J. et al. (2017), "A meta-analysis of class size and ratios in early childhood programs: Are thresholds of quality associated with greater impacts on cognitive, achievement, and socioemotional outcomes?", *Educational Evaluation and Policy Analysis*, advanced online publication, http://dx.doi.org/10.3102/0162373716689489.   [45]

Bradbury, B. et al. (2011), "Inequality during the Early Years: Child Outcomes and Readiness to Learn in Australia, Canada, United Kingdom, and United States", http://ftp.iza.org/dp6120.pdf (accessed on 15 February 2018).   [14]

Britto, P., H. Yoshikawa and K. Boller (2011), "Quality of early childhood development programs and policies in global contexts: Rationale for investment, conceptual framework and implications for equity", *Social Policy Report*, Vol. 25/2, pp. 1-31.   [1]

Burchinal, M. et al. (2002), "Caregiver training and classroom quality in child care centers", *Applied Developmental Science*, Vol. 6/1, pp. 2-11, http://dx.doi.org/10.1207/S1532480XADS0601_01.   [21]

Canadian Council on Learning (2006), "Why is High-Quality Child Care Essential? The Link between Quality Child Care and Early Learning", *Lessons in Learning*   [73]

Cardon, G. et al. (2008), "The contribution of preschool playground factors in explaining children's physical activity during recess", *International Journal of Behavioral Nutrition and Physical Activity*, Vol. 5/1, p. 11, http://dx.doi.org/10.1186/1479-5868-5-11.   [43]

Castle, S. et al. (2016), "Teacher-child interactions in early Head Start classrooms: Associations with teacher characteristics", *Early Education and Development*, Vol. 27/2, pp. 259-274, http://dx.doi.org/10.1080/10409289.2016.1102017.   [51]

Clarke-Stewart, K. et al. (2002), "Do regulable features of child-care homes affect children's development?", *Early Childhood Research Quarterly*, Vol. 17/1, pp. 52-86, http://dx.doi.org/10.1016/s0885-2006(02)00133-3.   [20]

Clifford, R. et al. (2005), "What is pre-kindergarten? Characteristics of public pre-kindergarten programs", *Applied Developmental Science*, Vol. 9/3, pp. 126-143, http://dx.doi.org/10.1207/s1532480xads0903_1.   [78]

Colwell, N. et al. (2013), "New evidence on the validity of the Arnett Caregiver Interaction Scale: Results from the early childhood longitudinal study-birth cohort", *Early Childhood Research Quarterly*, Vol. 28/2, pp. 218-233, http://dx.doi.org/10.1016/j.ecresq.2012.12.004.   [58]

de Haan, A. et al. (2013), "Targeted versus mixed preschools and kindergartens: Effects of class composition and teacher-managed activities on disadvanged children's emergent academic skills", *School Effectiveness and School Improvement: An International Journal of Research, Policy and Practice*, Vol. 24/2, pp. 177-194, http://dx.doi.org/10.1080/09243453.2012.749792.   [36]

de Schipper, E., J. Riksen-Walraven and S. Geurts (2007), "Multiple determinants of caregiver behavior in child care centers", *Early Childhood Research Quarterly*, Vol. 22/3, pp. 312-326, http://dx.doi.org/10.1016/j.ecresq.2007.04.004.   [17]

Dennis, S. and E. O'Connor (2013), "Reexamining Quality in Early Childhood Education: Exploring the Relationship Between the Organizational Climate and the Classroom", *Journal of Research in Childhood Education*, Vol. 27/1, pp. 74-92, http://dx.doi.org/10.1080/02568543.2012.739589.   [48]

Doherty, G. et al. (2006), "Predictors of quality in family child care", *Early Childhood Research Quarterly*, Vol. 21/3, pp. 296-312, http://dx.doi.org/10.1016/j.ecresq.2006.07.006.   [59]

Early, D. et al. (2006), "Are teachers' education, major, and credentials related to classroom quality and children's academic gains in pre-kindergarten?", *Early Childhood Research Quarterly*, Vol. 21/2, pp. 174-195, http://dx.doi.org/10.1016/j.ecresq.2006.04.004.   [57]

Early, D. et al. (2007), "Teachers' education, classroom quality, and young children's academic skills: Results from seven studies of preschool programs", *Child Development*, Vol. 78/2, pp. 558-580, http://dx.doi.org/ 10.1111/j.1467-8624.2007.01014.x.   [28]

Egert, F. (2015), *Meta-analysis on the impact of in-service professionals development programs for preschool teachers on quality ratings and child outcomes*, doctoral dissertation, Bamberg, Germany.   [72]

Elliott, A. (2006), "Early Childhood Education: Pathways to quality and equity for all children", *Australian Education Review*, Vol. 50.   [31]

Feinstein, L. (2003), "Inequality in the early cognitive development of British children in the 1970 cohort", *Economica*, Vol. 70/277, pp. 73-97, http://dx.doi.org/10.1111/1468-0335.t01-1-00272.   [15]

Fontaine, N. et al. (2006), "Increasing quality in early care and learning environments", *Early Child Development and Care*, Vol. 176/2, pp. 157-169, http://dx.doi.org/10.1080/0300443042000302690.   [29]

Fukkink, R. and A. Lont (2007), "Does training matter? A meta-analysis and review of caregiver training studies", *Early Childhood Research Quarterly*, Vol. 22, pp. 294-311, http://dx.doi.org/10.1016/j.ecresq.2007.04.005.   [63]

Hamre, B. et al. (2014), *Classroom Assessment Scoring System (CLASS) manual*, Paul H. Brookes Publishing Co.   [4]

Hamre, B. et al. (2012), "A course on effective teacher-child interactions: Effects on teacher beliefs, knowledge, and observed practice", *American Educational Research Journal*, Vol. 49/1, pp. 88-123, http://dx.doi.org/10.3102/0002831211434596.   [64]

Ho, D., M. Lee and Y. Teng (2016), "Size matters: The link between staff size and perceived organizational support in early childhood education", *International Journal of Educational Management*, Vol. 30/6, pp. 1104-1122, http://dx.doi.org/10.1108/IJEM-09-2015-0125.   [49]

Howes, C. (1997), "Children's experiences in center-based child care as a function of teacher background and adult:child ratio.", *Merrill-Palmer Quarterly*, Vol. 43, pp. 404-425.   [44]

Howes, C. et al. (2008), "Ready to learn? Children's pre-academic achievement in pre-Kindergarten programs", *Early Childhood Research Quarterly*, Vol. 23/1, pp. 27-50, http://dx.doi.org/10.1016/j.ecresq.2007.05.002.   [2]

Hulpia, H. et al. (2016), *MeMoQ Deelrapport 10. Emotionele en educatieve ondersteuning in de nulmeting*, Kind en Gezin, Ugent, KU Leuven.   [41]

Huntsman, L. (2008), *Determinants of quality in child care: A review of the research evidence*, Centre for Parenting and Research, Ashfield, NSW, http://www.community.nsw.gov.au/__data/assets/pdf_file/0020/321617/research_qualitychildcare.pdf.   [22]

Jeon, L., C. Buettner and E. Hur (2014), "Examining pre-school classroom quality in a statewide quality rating and improvement system", *Child & Youth Care Forum*, Vol. 43/4, pp. 469-487, http://dx.doi.org/10.1007/s10566-014-9248-z.   [74]

Justice, L. et al. (2008), "Quality of language and literacy instruction in preschool classrooms serving at-risk pupils", *Early Childhood Research Quarterly*, Vol. 23/1, pp. 51-68, http://dx.doi.org/10.1016/j.ecresq.2007.09.004.   [65]

King, E. et al. (2016), "Classroom quality in infant and toddler classrooms: impact of age and programme type", *Early Child Development and Care*, Vol. 186/11, pp. 1821-1835, http://dx.doi.org/10.1080/03004430.2015.1134521.   [52]

Lahti, M. et al. (2015), "Approaches to validating child care quality rating and improvement systems (QRIS): Results from two states with similar QRIS type", *Early Childhood Research Quarterly*, Vol. 30, pp. 280-290, http://dx.doi.org/10.1016/j.ecresq.2014.04.005.   [75]

Lipscomb, S. et al. (2017), *Oregon's quality rating improvement system (QRIS) validation study one: Associations with observed program quality*, Portland State University and Oregon State University.   [76]

Litjens, I. and M. Taguma (2010), *Literature overview for the 7th meeting of the OECD network on early childhood education and care*, OECD, Paris.   [27]

LoCassale-Crouch, J. et al. (2011), "Implementing an early childhood professional development course across 10 sites and 15 sections: Lessons learned", *NHSA Dialog: A Research-to-Practice Journal for the Early Childhood Field*, Vol. 14/4, pp. 275-292, http://dx.doi.org/10.1080/15240754.2011.617527.   [66]

Manlove, E. and J. Guzell (1997), "Intention to Leave, Anticipated Reasons for Leaving, and 12-Month Turnover of Child Care Center Staff", *Early Childhood Research Quarterly*, Vol. 12, pp. 145-167, http://10.1016/S0885-2006(97)90010-7 (accessed on 2 February 2018). [25]

Mashburn, A. et al. (2008), "Measures of classroom quality in prekindergarten and children's development of academic, language, and social skills", *Child Development*, Vol. 79/3, pp. 732-749, http://dx.doi.org/10.1111/j.1467-8624.2008.01154.x. [5]

Mitchell, L. and P. Cubey (2003), *Characteristics of professional development linked to enhanced pedagogy and children's learning in early childhood settings*, NCER. [38]

Moon, J. and J. Burbank (2004), "The Early Childhood Education Career and Wage Ladder: A Model for Improving Quality in Early Learning and Care Programs", http://www.eoionline.org (accessed on 2 February 2018). [23]

Murnane, R. et al. (1990), "The effects of salaries and opportunity costs on length of stay in teaching: Evidence from North Carolina", *Journal of Human Resources*, Vol. 25/1, pp. 106-124, https://econpapers.repec.org/article/uwpjhriss/v_3a25_3ay_3a1990_3ai_3a1_3ap_3a106-124.htm (accessed on 2 February 2018). [24]

NICHD Early Child Care Research Network (2002), "Child-care structure → process → outcome: Direct and indirect effects of child-care quality on young children's development", *Psychological Science*, Vol. 13/3, pp. 199-206, http://dx.doi.org/10.1111/1467-9280.00438. [46]

OECD (2018), *Education at a Glance 2018: OECD Indicators*, OECD Publishing, Paris, https://dx.doi.org/10.1787/eag-2018-en. [19]

OECD (2018), *Engaging Young Children: Lessons from Research about Quality in Early Childhood Education and Care*, Starting Strong, OECD Publishing, Paris, https://dx.doi.org/10.1787/9789264085145-en. [3]

OECD (2017), *Starting Strong 2017: Key OECD Indicators on Early Childhood Education and Care*, Starting Strong, OECD Publishing, Paris, https://dx.doi.org/10.1787/9789264276116-en. [18]

OECD (2017), *Starting Strong V: Transitions from Early Childhood Education and Care to Primary Education*, Starting Strong, OECD Publishing, Paris, https://dx.doi.org/10.1787/9789264276253-en. [8]

OECD (2015), *Starting Strong IV: Monitoring Quality in Early Childhood Education and Care*, Starting Strong, OECD Publishing, Paris, http://dx.doi.org/10.1787/9789264233515-en. [9]

OECD (2011), *Starting Strong III: A Quality Toolbox for Early Childhood Education and Care*, Starting Strong, OECD Publishing, Paris, https://dx.doi.org/10.1787/9789264123564-en. [11]

OECD (2006), *Starting Strong II: Early Childhood Education and Care*, Starting Strong, OECD Publishing, Paris, https://dx.doi.org/10.1787/9789264035461-en. [26]

Phillipsen, L. et al. (1997), "The prediction of process quality from structural features of child care", *Early Childhood Research Quarterly*, Vol. 12, pp. 281-303, http://dx.doi.org/10.1016/S0885-2006(97)90004-1. [30]

Pianta, R. et al. (2005), "Features of Pre-Kindergarten programs, classrooms, and teachers: Do they predict observed classroom quality and child-teacher interactions?", *Applied Developmental Science*, Vol. 9/3, pp. 144-159. [77]

Raikes, H., H. Raikes and B. Wilcox (2005), "Regulation, subsidy receipt and provide characteristics: What predicts quality in child care homes?", *Early Childhood Research Quarterly*, Vol. 20/2, pp. 164-184, http://dx.doi.org/10.1016/j.ecresq.2005.04.006. [60]

Sammons, P. (2010), *The EPPE Research Design: an educational effectiveness focus*, Routledge, London/New York. [34]

Schaack, D., V. Le and C. Setodji (2017), "Home-based child care provider education and specialized training: Associations with caregiving quality and toddler social-emotional and cognitive outcomes", *Early Education and Development*, Vol. 28/6, pp. 655-668, http://dx.doi.org/10.1080/10409289.2017.1321927. [61]

Scottish Government (2016), "Growing up in Scotland", http://hub.careinspectorate.com/media/355563/language-development-and-enjoyment-of-reading-impacts-of-early-parent-child-activities-in-two-growing-up-in-scotland-cohorts.pdf (accessed on 15 February 2018). [10]

Sheridan, S. (2001), "Quality Evaluation and Quality Enhancement in Preschool - A Model of Competence Development", *Early Child Development and Care*, Vol. 166, pp. 7-27. [37]

Sheridan, S. et al. (2009), "A cross-cultural study of preschool quality in South Korea and Sweden: ECERS evaluations", *Early Childhood Research Quarterly*, Vol. 24/2, pp. 142-156, http://dx.doi.org/10.1016/j.ecresq.2009.03.004. [32]

Shonkoff, J. and D. Phillips (2000), *From neurons to neighborhoods: The science of early childhood development*, National Academy Press.   [33]

Siraj-Blatchford, I. et al. (2005), "Technical Paper 10 "Intensive Case Studies of Practice Across Foundation Stage", http://www.leeds.ac.uk/educol/documents/00003934.htm (accessed on 19 February 2018).   [70]

Slot, P. (2017), *Literature review on Early Childhood Education and Care quality: Relations between structural characteristics at different levels and process quality*, Internal document, OECD, Paris.   [7]

Slot, P. et al. (2018), "Structural and Process Quality of Danish Preschools: Direct and Indirect Associations With Children's Growth in Language and Preliteracy Skills", *Early Education and Development*, Vol. 29/4, pp. 581-602, http://dx.doi.org/10.1080/10409289.2018.1452494.   [67]

Slot, P. et al. (2017), "Measurement properties of the CLASS Toddler in ECEC in the Netherlands", *Journal of Applied Developmental Psychology*, Vol. 48, pp. 79-91, http://dx.doi.org/10.1016/j.appdev.2016.11.008.   [6]

Slot, P., M. Lerkkanen and P. Leseman (2015), *The relations between structural quality and process quality in European early childhood education and care provisions: Secondary data analyses of large scale studies in five countries*, CARE, http://ecec-care.org/fileadmin/careproject/Publications/reports/CARE_WP2_D2__2_Secondary_data_analyses.pdf.   [68]

Slot, P. et al. (2015), "Associations between structural quality aspects and process quality in Dutch early childhood education and care settings", *Early Childhood Research Quarterly*, Vol. 33, pp. 64-76, http://dx.doi.org/10.1016/j.ecresq.2015.06.001.   [53]

Sylva, K. et al. (2004), *The Effective Provision of Pre-school Education (EPPE) project: Final Report - A longitudinal study funded by the DfES 1997-2004*, Institute of Education, University of London/ Department for Education and Skills/ Sure Start, London.   [16]

Sylva, K., I. Siraj-Blatchford and B. Taggart (2003), *Assessing quality in the early years: Early Childhood Environmental Rating Scale Extension (ECERS-E) four curricular subscales*, Trentham Books, London.   [12]

Thomason, A. and K. La Paro (2009), "Measuring the quality of teacher–child interactions in toddler child care", *Early Education and Development*, Vol. 20, pp. 285-304, http://dx.doi.org/10.1080/10409280902773351.   [54]

van Voorhis, F. et al. (2013), "The Impact of Family Involvement on the Education of Children Ages 3 to 8: A Focus on Literacy and Math Achievement Outcomes and Social-Emotional Skills - Executive Summary", https://www.mdrc.org/sites/default/files/The_Impact_of_Family_Imvolvement_ES.pdf (accessed on 15 February 2018).   [13]

Vandenbroeck, M. et al. (2018), *Quality in family child care providers: A study of variations in process quality of home-based childcare*, Submitted for publication in European Early Childhood Education Journal.   [62]

Vogel, C. et al. (2015), *Toddlers in early Head Start: A portrait of 2-years-olds, their families, and the program serving them*, Office of Planning, Research and Evaluation, Administration for Children and Families, U.S. Department of Health and Human Services, Washington, DC.   [55]

Vogel, C. et al. (2015), *Toddlers in early Head Start: A portrait of 3-years-olds, their families, and the program serving them*, Office of Planning, Research and Evaluation, Administration for Children and Families, U.S. Department of Health and Human Services, Washington, DC.   [56]

von Suchodoletz, A. et al. (2017), *"Associations among quality indicators in early childhood education and care (ECEC) and relations with child development and learning: A meta-analysis"*, Internal document, OECD, Paris.   [39]

Zaslow, M. et al. (2010), *Quality, dosage, thresholds, and features in early childhood settings: A review of the literature*, Mathematica Policy Research, Washington, DC.   [69]

Zaslow, M. et al. (2004), "The role of professional development in creating high quality preschool education", *Welfare Reform & Beyond Working Paper*, https://www.brookings.edu/wp-content/uploads/2016/06/200411Zaslow.pdf (accessed on 19 February 2018).   [71]

POLICIES FOR EARLY LEARNING: SHAPING PEDAGOGY

This chapter reviews approaches to pedagogical practice in early childhood education and care, with a view to enhancing the knowledge, skills, attitudes and values that are central to success in the 21st century. It then looks at policies that support such pedagogies. The chapter concludes with a review of approaches to curriculum design that can facilitate a smooth transition from early learning to school.

A note regarding Israel
The statistical data for Israel are supplied by and under the the responsibility of the relevant Israeli authorities. The use of such data by the OECD is without prejudice to the status of the Golan Heights, East Jerusalem and Israeli settlements in the West Bank under the terms of international law.

Pedagogy is at the heart of teaching and learning. Preparing children to become lifelong learners with a deep knowledge of subject matter and a broad set of social skills requires understanding how pedagogy influences learning. Doing so shifts the perception of teachers from technicians who strive to attain the education goals set by the curriculum to experts in the science and art of teaching. Seen through this lens, innovation in teaching becomes a problem-solving process rooted in teachers' professionalism, a response to the daily challenges of constantly changing classrooms. The research on pedagogy and policy for early childhood education and care cited in this chapter is mostly drawn from the *Early Childhood Education and Care Pedagogy Review: England* (Wall, Litjens and Taguma, 2015[1]), the report, *Starting Strong V: Transitions from Early Childhood Education and Care to Primary Education* (OECD, 2017[2]), and the conceptual framework of the OECD *Starting Strong Teaching and Learning International Survey* (Sim, M. et al., forthcoming[3]).

APPROACHES TO PEDAGOGICAL PRACTICE IN EARLY CHILDHOOD EDUCATION AND CARE

A distinction is often drawn between child-centred instruction (activities are child-initiated, children engage in problem solving and enquiry-oriented learning) and didactic instruction (staff-directed, planned tasks focusing on acquiring and practicing academic skills), although in practice these approaches need not be distinct. Both approaches may boost children's skills, and practitioners could combine different approaches depending on the purpose; but some evidence suggests the importance of including child-centred instruction at the earliest ages (Huffman and Speer, 2000[4]). Academic, teacher-directed approaches generally have clearly defined, specific aims and strategies. This can be an advantage for practitioners, since they are easier to apply. They may also make it easier to monitor children's development, and conduct staff self-evaluations.

Ensuring child-centred approaches are included in early childhood pedagogies can give children choices and opportunities for autonomy and may promote children's socio-emotional abilities, such as self-regulation and self-control. These are believed to be crucial for development and success as children progress through education. Policy documents and studies generally recommend combining both approaches and practices to stimulate early development.

OECD's work on early childhood education and care reflect a consensus view that can be characterised as social-constructivist, which stresses the importance of children's intrinsically motivated activity and initiative as the engine of development (McMullen et al., 2005[5]; Pramling-Samuelsson and Fleer, 2009[6]), but acknowledges that development does not take place in a cultural void. The role of early childhood education and care staff, therefore, is not confined to creating conditions for optimal self-propelled development; staff should also deliberately introduce children to cultural domains, such as emergent skills in language, literacy, numeracy, mathematics and science. However, how this is carried out should respect developmental and motivational principles. This consensus is reflected in the concept of "developmentally appropriate practice" coined by early childhood education specialist Sue Bredekamp (Bredekamp, 1987[7]).

That said, early childhood education and care programmes still differ in emphasis. Pressure to achieve immediate results in easily measurable domains, such as literacy and mathematics, can undermine the developmental approach and lead to a more didactic approach (Dickinson, 2002[8]; Marcon, 2002[9]). Some approaches to early childhood education and care pedagogy stress the importance of the staff-directed transmission of knowledge and skills related to the curriculum. This may also result in a highly didactic approach, with limited use of child-centred pedagogies, even with very young children, where direct instruction and rewards are used to reinforce learning processes with the aim of preparing children for primary school.

Pedagogical approaches and the development of academic, social and emotional skills

Research on different pedagogical focuses (Barnett et al., 2010[10]; Eurydice, 2009[11]; Laevers, 2011[12]; Schweinhart and Weikart, 1997[13]) indicates that both staff-initiated and child-initiated practices consist of elements that can be used to develop comprehensive and effective early childhood education and care programmes (Table 3.2). Academic, staff-initiated practices and approaches are more likely to improve children's academic outcomes, including IQ scores, literacy and numeracy skills, and specific subject knowledge, and are most likely to have short-term outcomes. Child-centred practices are more likely to improve a child's socio-emotional and soft skills, such as motivation to learn, creativity, independence, self-confidence, general knowledge and initiative, and have long-term outcomes. Research also cautions that strong, didactic, staff-directed practices may hinder the development of children's socio-emotional skills, such as motivation, interest and self-regulation, in the long run. See, for example (Burts et al., 1992[14]; Haskins, 1985[15]; Stipek et al., 1995[16]).

A Finnish study (Lerkkanen et al., 2012[17]) looked at kindergarten (6-year-olds) teaching practices and children's interest in reading and mathematics. It found that children were more interested in mathematics and reading when child-centred instruction was prioritised. Similarly, instruction that blended child-initiated and staff-directed instruction led to higher levels of school readiness and early school achievement (Graue et al., 2004[18]).

Early childhood education and care programmes for low-income and ethnic minority children using direct academic instruction have been reported to be effective in obtaining desired cognitive and academic goals (Dickinson, 2011[19]; Gersten, Walker and Darch, 1988[20]; Justice et al., 2008[21]; Schweinhart and Weikart, 1997[13]). Focusing on children primarily from low-income and minority families, (Marcon, 1999[22]) compared three preschool approaches for their effect on children's development and mastery of language, literacy and mathematics at the end of preschool. The results revealed that children who attended a child-centred preschool that followed developmentally appropriate practice demonstrated greater mastery of basic skills at the end of preschool than children in programmes using a didactic approach. However, the advantage of child-centred over academic preschools was small, and both programmes had far better results than a mixed-model approach that combined elements of both. In a follow-up study, a more complex picture was found. Marcon (Marcon, 1999[22]) concluded that children from child-centred and mixed preschools were better prepared to face new challenges in grade four.

In another study, Stipek et al. (Stipek et al., 1995[16]) found that although children in didactic, teacher-directed programmes showed better skills in a letters/reading achievement test than children enrolled in child-centred programmes, they showed relatively negative outcomes on most of the socio-emotional measures, including dependency on adults, self-esteem, and beliefs in their own accomplishments. In line with those findings, Goldberg (Goldberg, 2000[23]) stressed that children in more academically oriented preschool programmes do better in achievement tests, since that is the focus of academically oriented approaches, but that child-centred preschool programmes enhance children's socio-emotional development. In general, children in such programmes show greater self-efficacy, less dependency on adults, more pride in their own accomplishments, and have less concern about school later on. Since socio-emotional development is found to be related to later academic success (e.g. self-regulation), this area is important to include in early childhood education and care.

Critical to the issue of developmental versus didactic approaches is whether programme effects are assessed in the short or long term. Schweinhart and Weikart (Schweinhart and Weikart, 1997[13]) compared the High/Scope curriculum[1] with a didactic, basic skills-oriented programme and a traditional approach, characterised as "laissez faire". In the short term, the didactic programme and the High/Scope curriculum were equally effective in the cognitive domain. But over the long term, additional advantages of the High/Scope curriculum became evident, with better self-regulation, work attitude, motivation, and social and behavioural adjustment resulting in superior social outcomes in adulthood (e.g. less crime, more economic independence) compared to the other approaches. These later social outcomes are similar to those reported for the Perry Preschool Project, the predecessor of the High/Scope curriculum.

The evidence suggests that a developmental approach provides a strong educational foundation for young children, whereas older preschool children should be gradually prepared for the learning tasks they will encounter in primary school. An academic orientation on basic knowledge and skills (for instance, concerning phonological awareness and letter knowledge) can be embedded in a curriculum of playful activities in small groups, including episodes of shared dialogical reading and talking, with the early childhood education and care staff, to foster children's vocabulary, comprehension skills and world knowledge (Bus, Leseman and Neuman, 2012[24]; Dickinson et al., 2003[25]).

A later emphasis on academic knowledge and skills after a predominantly developmental approach may provide better support for the transition to primary school. Evidence for such an age effect is reported by Stipek et al. (Stipek et al., 1998[26]) who compared four groups of mainly low-income and ethnic minority children attending either a developmentally appropriate-practice preschool or a basic skills-oriented preschool from age 3 to 5, and after preschool, either a developmental or a basic skills-oriented kindergarten from age 5 to 6, before starting primary school. The results indicated that a developmentally appropriate-practice curriculum in preschool up to age 5 produced positive developmental effects in both academic and social-emotional domains, regardless of the type of kindergarten attended in the third year. However, a greater academic focus in kindergarten (age 5 to 6) after two years in a developmentally appropriate practice-focused preschool, had slightly better learning outcomes in primary school, and no negative social-emotional outcomes compared to programmes with a continued focus on developmentally appropriate practice. The latter programmes were slightly better for problem solving and language comprehension.

Table 3.1

Overview of pedagogical approaches and practices and their effects

Pedagogical approach/practice	Description	Effects
Play-based learning	Different forms of "play-based learning". Traditionally, free-play activities are initiated and freely chosen by the child.	• Some play activities, such as puzzles and games, are more engaging than others, for example playing in sand and dressing up. • Play partners and sensitive adults are important to help children reflect on play situations and understand what they have learnt. • The role of practitioners in play situations is important. In high-quality situations, adults listen to and extend children's thoughts and knowledge.
Sustained shared thinking	"Two or more individuals work together in an interrelated way to solve a problem, clarify a concept, evaluate an activity, etc." (Siraj-Blatchford et al., 2012)	• Children have been noted to make greater progress generally in settings where more sustained shared thinking took place.
Scaffolding	Involves helpful, structured interaction between an adult and a child, with the aim of helping the child achieve a specific goal.	• Children in scaffolding-focused learning environments demonstrated in one study greater overall positive effects on their development than children in teacher-directed and children-centred environments.
Child-directed	Method of learning that prioritises child-initiated activities, i.e. activities that are chosen by the child. Few staff-initiated activities.	• Child-directed practices are likely to improve children's socio-emotional and soft skills, such as their motivation to learn, creativity, independence, self-confidence, general knowledge and initiative.
Teacher(staff)-directed	Classic method of learning with activities mainly initiated by the teacher, which include frequent repetition.	• French children taught in chiefly teacher-led environments performed better on spatial organisation and rhythm tests than German children from child-centred environments. • Marcon (2002) concluded that the development of children who are teacher-led at the early childhood education and care stage is slowed because the introduction of formalised learning experiences is too early for children's developmental status at this age.

Sources: Anders (2015); Dohrmann et al. (2007) ; Dunn and Kontos (1997) ; Haan, Elbers and Leseman (2004); Lilliard (2012); Lilliard and Else-Quest (2006); Miller (1975); AEYC (2009); Schmidt et al. (2007); Siraj-Blatchford et al. (2002); Stipek et al. (1995); Sylva et al. (2004).

SHAPING PEDAGOGY THROUGH POLICY

A key policy lever influencing pedagogy is the curriculum. All the cases studied for the OECD *Early Childhood Education and Care Pedagogy Review: England* (Wall, Litjens and Taguma, 2015[1]) have some form of curriculum or framework set at the national level, and its prescribed learning areas and goals influence the pedagogical approaches and practices early childhood education and care providers espouse.

Curricula specify what is valued at a particular level of education, potentially including learning objectives, content, methods (including assessment) and materials for teaching and learning, in addition to arrangements for teacher training and professional development (OECD, 2018[27]; Sylva et al., 2016[28]). A curriculum framework is an overarching document that articulates the scope of a curriculum within the broader context of the education system. Curriculum frameworks often provide principles to help staff organise their pedagogical work to address developmental goals or learning standards (OECD, 2018[27]).

The curricula for early childhood education and care often contrast with those used in primary schooling, partly because the latter tend to focus on the content to be taught, while the former typically rely on psychological and educational theories that inform pedagogical practice, i.e. how to teach, rather than what to teach (Frede and Ackerman, 2007[29]).

Most OECD countries have designed and implemented curricula for early childhood education and care services, especially for ISCED 02 (OECD, 2011[30]), and adoption of such curricula is increasingly accepted (Bertrand, 2007[31]). But there is still strong debate about what constitutes appropriate curricula and pedagogy for younger children (Chazan-Cohen et al., 2017[32]; Sylva et al., 2016[28]).

The literature on early childhood education and care curricula highlights the importance of children engaging in experiential and relational activities. Research shows that child-centred practice and small-group activities that allow children to engage in active discussions and interactions are associated with higher process quality in early learning settings (Sylva et al., 2016[28]). Curriculum implementation can be considered an aspect of process quality.

In early childhood education and care, a constructivist approach is often the preferred curriculum model as it advocates the importance of attending to children's overall development (Copple and Bredekamp, 2009[33]; Frede and Ackerman, 2007[29]). This is based, in part, on research showing that the economic benefits associated with attending high-quality preschool programmes (e.g. better labour-market and health outcomes, among others, in adulthood) come from a combination of socio-emotional and academic competencies (Boyd et al., 2005[34]; Frede and Ackerman, 2007[29]). Yet, there is a wide variety of designs and focus of these curricula. Often, early childhood education and care curricula are described as whole-child, holistic curricula or as skill-specific curricula (Boyd et al., 2005[34]; Frede and Ackerman, 2007[29]). The first emphasises a child-centred approach and tends to be associated with the arrangement of the classroom and materials to promote active learning. Skill-specific curricula, by contrast, focus on promoting learning in specific areas, including academic (particularly literacy and mathematics) and socio-emotional skills (Jenkins and Duncan, 2017[35]). These curricula are often influenced by standards set to measure child development and learning; as such, they reflect a more structuralist approach to teaching and learning.

However, in practice, the dichotomy between holistic and skill-specific curricula is not always relevant. That is, even when curricula include a specific focal area, they can also promote child-centred, active learning and children's development in areas beyond the focal domain (Weiland et al., 2018[36]). Conversely, curricula that take a more holistic approach without specifying focal content areas can also contribute to children's learning and development in specific areas (Marshall, 2017[37]). The effects of curricula can be difficult to evaluate given their influences (intended or otherwise) on both specific and global aspects of child development, and their importance for short-term learning gains and longer-term well-being. How curricula are implemented appears to be of central importance for children's learning, development and well-being.

The overlap of and similarities between skills-specific and holistic curricula notwithstanding, research in Europe shows that holistic, child-centred curricula with a recognition that children learn through play are predominant (Sylva, Ereky-Stevens and Aricescu, 2015[38]). This finding is consistent with that in countries outside of Europe, including the United States (NAEYC/NAECS-SDE, 2003[39]), New Zealand (New Zealand Ministry of Education, 2017[40]), Australia (DEEWR, 2010[41]), Canada (Ontario Government, 2007[42]), Japan (Ministry of Education, Culture, Sports, Science and Technology, Japan, 2017[43]) and in Latin America and the Caribbean (Harris-Van Keuren and Rodríguez Gómez, 2013[44]). There also appears to be a shared understanding that a curriculum for early childhood education and care should set common goals within an open framework, providing a good balance between education and care aimed at promoting children's development, well-being and learning. The values of this type of approach to curriculum are generally shared by parents, staff and policy makers (Moser et al., 2017[45]).

As discussed above, policies determining the qualifications, and the education and training of staff can also affect pedagogical approaches (Table 3.2). Practitioners need a number of professional competences and skills to be able to offer high-quality learning opportunities for young children. England has emphasised this issue. Higher staff qualifications are now expected, such as the requirement that one educator in an early childhood education and care setting must have Early Years Professional status. France demonstrates the influence of qualifications on pedagogical approaches and practices in another way. Teachers in both primary schools and preschool settings in France have the same qualifications and training, and similar pedagogical approaches are used in both settings. Questions remain as to how appropriate primary school pedagogy is in preschool settings, given children's levels of learning and development. This is particularly relevant for England, given the push to employ primary teachers in early childhood education and care.

Table 3.2

Key pedagogical approaches and practices in case-study countries

	Key Pedagogical Approaches	Main features	What evidence are pedagogical approaches and practices based on?	Which policies direct or affect pedagogical approaches?
United Kingdom	Child-centred	Adults provide a stimulating yet open-ended environment for children to play within.	Research Effective Pedagogy in the Early Years (REPEY - 2002) Early Years Foundation Stage Review (2011)	The Early Years Foundation Stage (EYFS), the Early Years National Curriculum Staff qualifications Monitoring and Quality Assurance: Ofsted inspections
	Teacher-directed	Teacher initiated, programmed learning approach.		
	Constructivist/ Interactive Approach	Views learning as an active exchange between the child and environment that progresses in 'stages', with adults and peers providing important stimulus in learning.		
	Play-based	Guided play opportunities are offered to children.		
	Sustained shared thinking	Two individuals work together in an intellectual way to perform activities such as solving a problem or clarifying a concept - both parties must contribute to the thinking and develop and extend it.		
	Scaffolding	Process in which the child is seen as a learner, rather than passive entity, and the adult acts respectfully, allowing the child to enter 'flow' a period of high concentrated play.		
Japan	Guiding Child Care Theory	Children learn best when they feel 'free' and are supported by the teacher in a sympathetic way.	Inspiration drawn from Montessori, Reggio Emilia, and Developmentally Appropriate Practice.	Course of Study for Kindergartens/ Guidelines for Nursery Care at Day Nurseries Staff qualifications Monitoring and Quality Assurance: external and internal evaluations
	Theory of three activities in preschool (play-based)	1. Activities comprise of free play and guidance aimed at developing daily life skills. 2. Elements are extracted from child's play and re-constructed to be educational. 3. Directly teach linguistic, mathematical or artistic concepts and skills.		
France	Didactic Pedagogy/ Direct Instruction	Classic method of learning with mainly teacher-initiated activities including repetition.	The theories and ideas of Piaget, Vgotsky and Bruner. Recent research studies on for example effective literacy, numeracy and phonology practices	National Curriculum Staff qualifications Monitoring and Quality Assurance: National and local inspections Alignment with formal schooling
	Constructivist/ Interactive Approach	Views learning as an active exchange between the child and environment that progresses in 'stages', with adults and peers providing important stimulus in learning. Learning is organised so that it constantly builds on what has already been taught.		
Denmark	Child-centred	Adults provide a stimulating yet open-ended environment for children to play within.		Curriculum Staff qualifications Parent Board
	Socio-pedagogic	Emphasis on dialogue between adults and children, as well as creative activities with discussions and reflections.		

   HELPING OUR YOUNGEST TO LEARN AND GROW: POLICIES FOR EARLY LEARNING

Table 3.2

Key pedagogical approaches and practices in case-study countries *(cont.)*

	Key Pedagogical Approaches	Main features	What evidence are pedagogical approaches and practices based on?	Which policies direct or affect pedagogical approaches?
Germany	Situation-orientated	Emphasis on learning in social situations, mainly play-based.	Theoretical ideas from Friere, Robinson, Zimmer. Pedagogical approaches from Humbolt, Fröbel, Montessori, Piaget. Statistical evaluations and qualitiative research on effective practices, particularly language stimulation.	Curriculum Staff qualifications Parent Board
	Constructivist/ Interactive Approach	Views learning as an active exchange between the child and environment that progresses in 'stages', with adults and peers providing important stimulus in learning. Learning is organised do that it constantly builds on what has already been taught.		
	Sustained shared thinking	Two individuals work together in an intellectual way to perform activities such as solving a problem or clarifying a concept - both parties must contribute to the thinking and develop and extend it.		
	Child-centred	Adults provide a stimulating yet open-ended environment for children to play within.		
New Zealand	Te Whãriki	Adopts a specific socio-cultural perspective that acknowledges the different culutral and social contexts in New Zealand. A social and interactive way of learning is highly important.	Te Ao Māori (the Maori culture) Pedagogical approaches and theories from Vygotsky, Bronfenbrenner, Rogoff. Priorities for Children's Learning in Early Childhood Services: Good Practice	Curriculum Staff qualifications Monitoring and Quality Assurance: National inspections and internal self-review

Sources: Anders, Y. (2015), *Literature Review on Pedagogy*, OECD Publishing, Paris; OECD (2014), "Survey on pedagogy", internal document, OECD, Paris.

POLICIES TO FACILITATE TRANSITIONS FROM PRE-PRIMARY TO PRIMARY EDUCATION

The transition from early childhood education and care to primary school is a major step for children and one that curriculum continuity can facilitate. Well-managed transitions are important because they can support child well-being, ensure that the benefits of early childhood education and care endure, prepare children for school and improve equity in education outcomes (OECD, 2017[2]). Furthermore, continuous and aligned curricula aim to provide students with consistent, progressive and holistic support for their development and learning processes (OECD, 2017[2]). By integrating or aligning curricula across early childhood education and care, and primary school, governments can support continuity for young children while simultaneously promoting progress and setting strong foundations for later stages of education. At the same time, concerns about "schoolification" and age-appropriate practice need to be considered as curricula converge across levels.

Although the curriculum is an important tool to support transitions, there is not necessarily one best approach to the alignment and/or integration of curricula for supporting children's learning and well-being. In addition, the contexts of individual education systems – including the organisation of the system, governance and division of responsibilities, professional continuity for staff and teachers and the over-arching goals of the education system – need to be considered.

CURRICULUM ALIGNMENT BETWEEN PRE-PRIMARY AND PRIMARY

Curricula commonly follow the organisation of education systems within respective jurisdictions. Looking across the 63 jurisdictions that participated in the OECD survey on transitions as well as the 7 case studies, the OECD Starting Strong V report found that curricula frameworks appear to be the rule for primary education (ISCED 1) and preschool (ISCED 02), while curricula for children under age 3 are less common(see Table 2.5 and Annex B (OECD, 2017[2]).

A recently published OECD working paper on curriculum alignment and progression between early childhood education and care and primary school shows the spectrum of alignment and integration between the two education levels (Shuey et al., 2019[46]).

In Japan and New Jersey (United States), different curriculum frameworks are used for early childhood education and care, on the one hand, and primary school, on the other. However, in both places, efforts are underway to align aspects of the curricula or learning standards, or otherwise provide continuity between the two levels of education. For example, in Japan, the use of the "Start" curricula aims to provide continuity from early childhood education and care during the first months of primary school. New Jersey also promotes continuity in learning standards and pre-service professional development from the pre-primary level through third grade in primary school. New Zealand and Norway have explicitly aligned models, with different curricula for early childhood education and care and primary school. In these cases, there is an explicit connection between the frameworks, in content, pedagogy and/or development goals. For instance, in Norway, the Framework Plan for the Content and Tasks of Kindergartens defines learning areas in ways similar to those in the country's primary school curriculum. An example of a fully integrated curriculum is Scotland's Curriculum for Excellence, which covers education for children aged 3 to 18. Luxembourg and Victoria (Australia) have integrated curricula too, although these cover a narrower age range than that in Scotland. Table 3.3 provides a more detailed overview of the organisation of curricula in the seven jurisdictions studied.

Table 3.3

Curriculum organisation in seven jurisdictions

	Curriculum ISCED 01	Curriculum ISCED 02	Curriculum ISCED 1
Japan	National Curriculum Standards for Day care Centres (0 5 years) National Curriculum Standards for Integrated Centres for ECEC (0 5 years)		National Curriculum Standards for Elementary Schools (6-12 years)
		National Curriculum Standards for Kindergarten (35 years)	
Luxembourg		Curriculum Framework for Pre-primary and Primary Education (312 years)	
	National Framework for Non-formal Education of Children and Young People (0-12 years)		
New Jersey (United States)	New Jersey Early Learning Pathways (05 years) Preschool Implementation Guidelines Kindergarten Implementation Guidelines		New Jersey Student Learning Standards (5-18 years) 1st-3rd-grade Implementation Guide
New Zealand	*Te Whāriki* (Early childhood curriculum) (0-5 years)		New Zealand Curriculum and *Te Marautanga o Aotearoa*.(the national curriculum for Māori medium schooling) (618 years)
Norway	Framework Plan for the Content and Tasks of Kindergartens (0- 5 years)		The Knowledge Promotion Curriculum (6 18 years)
Scotland (United Kingdom)		Curriculum for Excellence (CfE) (318 years)	
Victoria (Australia)	Victorian Early Years Learning and Development Framework (VEYLDF) (08 years)		
			Victorian Curriculum F-10 (517 years)

Source: Shuey, E. et al. (2019), "Curriculum alignment and progression between early childhood education and care and primary school: A brief review and case studies", *OECD Education Working Papers*, OECD Publishing, Paris.

Other examples of integrated curricula include Italy, the same curriculum covers the education of children between the ages of 3 and 14. By contrast, Wales (United Kingdom) has an integrated curriculum that covers a shorter period but still spans early childhood education and care, and the beginning of primary education, for children aged 3 to 7. As shown in Figure 3.1, 78% of jurisdictions (46 out of 59) reported having curricula aligned between the last year of early childhood education and care, and the first year of primary school. In 24% of the jurisdictions (14 out of 59), the curriculum framework for the last year of early childhood education and care was also fully integrated with the primary school curriculum (OECD, 2017[2]).

Figure 3.2 shows the types of content in curriculum frameworks in jurisdictions that reported alignment between early childhood education and care, and primary school. Values and principles, and pedagogical approaches are the most common areas of alignment (OECD, 2017[2]).

Figure 3.1

Percentage of jurisdictions where early childhood and primary education curricula are either aligned or integrated (2016)

Based on information from 59 countries and jurisdictions

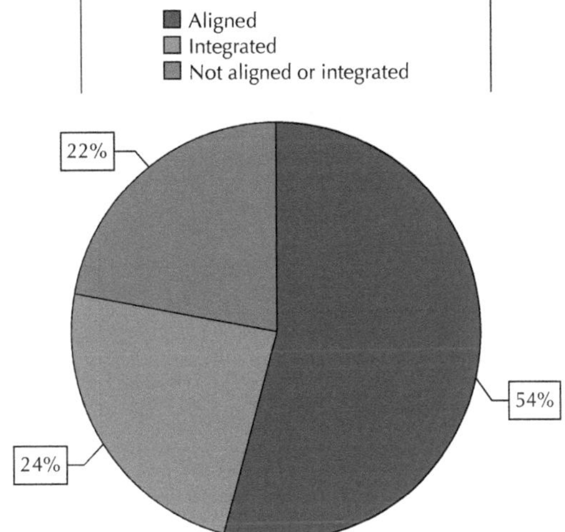

Source: OECD (2017), *Starting Strong V: Transitions from Early Childhood Education and Care to Primary Education,* Starting Strong, OECD Publishing, Paris, https://dx.doi.org/10.1787/9789264276253-en.

Figure 3.2

Values and principles included in both early childhood and primary education curricula (2016)

Based on information from 54 countries and jurisdictions

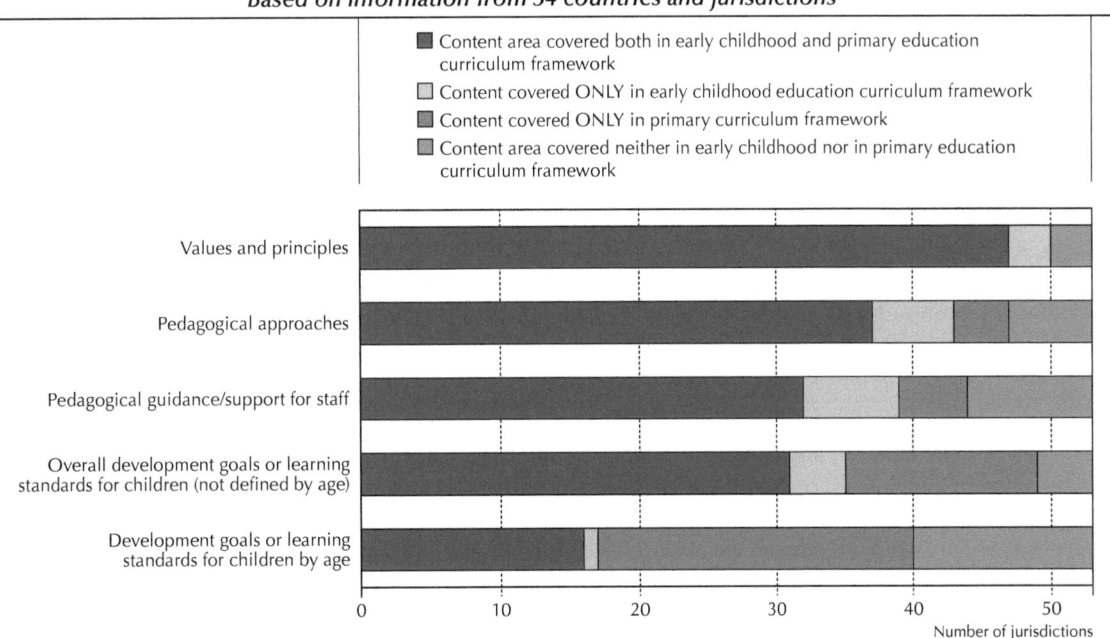

Note: Jurisdictions reported the curricular content during the first year of early childhood education and care and the first year of primary school. Three jurisdictions were excluded from the comparisons: For Canada (Nunavut): Curriculum Foundations does not cover specific areas or topics, but rather is an overarching curriculum document. Elementary Teacher's Planning Guide does not cover specific areas. Canada (Quebec): Accueillir la petite enfance. Le programme éducatif des services de garde du Québec does not cover specific subjects or areas, but addresses the global development of a child. New Zealand: Te Whāriki does not prescribe individual subject areas. The curriculum contains a set of interwoven principles, goals and strands that serves as the basis for curriculum implementation.
Source: OECD (2017), *Starting Strong V: Transitions from Early Childhood Education and Care to Primary Education,* Starting Strong, OECD Publishing, Paris, https://dx.doi.org/10.1787/9789264276253-en.

There are a number of policy approaches to support children's transitions from early childhood education and care to primary school (Table 3.3). For instance, in Finland, in order to address a lack of pedagogical continuity, revisions were made to curricular documents for early childhood education and care and for primary education by transforming traditional primary school subjects into more general learning areas, especially during the first two years of primary education (OECD, 2017[2]).

Table 3.4

Ensuring pedagogical continuity: Challenges and strategies

Challenges	Strategies

• Differences and inconsistencies in curricula:
 	
  • Inconsistent attention to transition across curricular documents (Norway)
 	
  • Differing emphases on goals and focus of education (care) in curricular documents (Slovenia)
 	
  • Decentralised distribution of responsibility for early childhood education and care and primary education (Austria and Finland)
	• Develop an integrated curriculum framework and national guidelines (Austria, Ireland, Slovenia)
	
	• Invest in local knowledge and innovations (Sweden)

• Lack of shared pedagogical understanding between the two systems (Finland, Norway, Slovenia)	• Reform curricula to ensure greater pedagogical continuity (Japan, Finland, New Zealand, Portugal, Scotland [United Kingdom], Sweden) • Provide opportunities for staff collaboration across levels (Japan, New Jersey [United States], Norway, Portugal, Wales [United Kingdom]) • Emphasise the role of primary school in receiving children (Norway, Portugal, Sweden)
• Inconsistent delivery of pedagogy during the transition from early childhood education and care to primary school (Denmark, Wales [United Kingdom])	• Ensure consistency in structures (Denmark) • Create collaborative learning strategies (Wales [United Kingdom])

Source: Adapted from OECD (2017), *Starting Strong V: Transitions from Early Childhood Education and Care to Primary Education*, Starting Strong, OECD Publishing, Paris, https://dx.doi.org/10.1787/9789264276253-en.

LEARNING AREAS IN EARLY CHILDHOOD EDUCATION AND CARE, AND PRIMARY SCHOOL CURRICULA

A comparison of two early childhood education and care policy surveys in 2011 and 2015 suggests a broadening of pre-primary (ISCED 02) curricula in 24 jurisdictions. A number of jurisdictions added health and well-being, social sciences, ethics and citizenship, information and communication technology (ICT) skills and foreign languages as learning areas during this period (Figure3.4). Notable increases were seen in the number of jurisdictions covering ethics and citizenship, from 17% of jurisdictions (4 out of 24) to almost 80% (19 out of 24), ICT skills, from 8% (2 out of 24) to 42% (10 out of 24) and those covering foreign languages, from 4% (1 out of 24) to 38% (9 out of 24). This broadening of pre-primary curricula suggests increasing alignment between pre-primary and primary curricula (OECD, 2017[2]).

In general, learning areas of early childhood education and care relate more to child well-being and less to specific learning content, which is more commonly included in primary school curricula, as shown in Figure 3.3. In New Zealand, *Te Whāriki* (the early childhood education curriculum) and the New Zealand Curriculum (for schools) share alignment at a high level. Furthermore, the 2017 update of *Te Whāriki* links its learning outcomes with key competencies and learning areas in the New Zealand Curriculum and *Te Marautanga o Aotearoa*, the curriculum for Māori-medium schools (Bell, 2017[47]). Learning goals and outcomes for young children are described more broadly, embedded in the five strands of *Te Whāriki* (well-being, belonging, contribution, communication and exploration), while learning areas for school-aged children are described through traditional academic disciplines: English; the arts; health and physical education; learning languages; mathematics and statistics; science; social sciences; and technology (New Zealand Ministry of Education, 2007[48]).

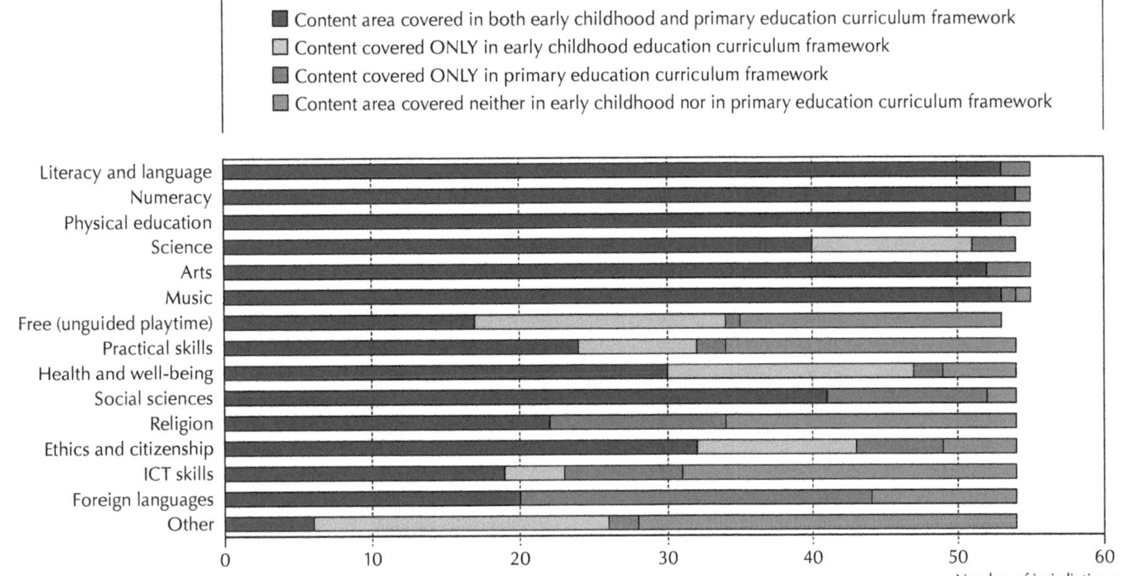

Note: Jurisdictions reported the curricular content during the first year of early childhood education and the first year of primary education. For jurisdictions where only one curriculum exists for early childhood and primary education, content was counted as "content area covered in both early childhood and primary education curriculum framework".

"Other" includes individual content named by the jurisdictions that fell outside the predetermined content, e.g. social skills and media; media and external activities; and safety.

Three jurisdictions were excluded from the comparisons:

• Canada (Nunavut): Curriculum Foundations does not cover specific areas or topics, but rather is an overarching curriculum document. The Elementary Teacher's Planning Guide does not cover specific areas.

• Canada (Quebec): Acceuillir la petite enfance. Le programme éducatif des services de garde du Québec does not cover specific subjects or areas but addresses the global development of a child.

• New Zealand: Te Whāriki does not prescribe individual subject areas. The curriculum contains a set of interwoven principles, goals and strands that serve as the basis for curriculum implementation.

Source: OECD (2017), *Starting Strong V: Transitions from Early Childhood Education and Care to Primary Education,* Starting Strong, OECD Publishing, Paris, https://dx.doi.org/10.1787/9789264276253-en.

Figure 3.4

Broadening pre-primary curricula to include emerging learning content (2011 and 2015)

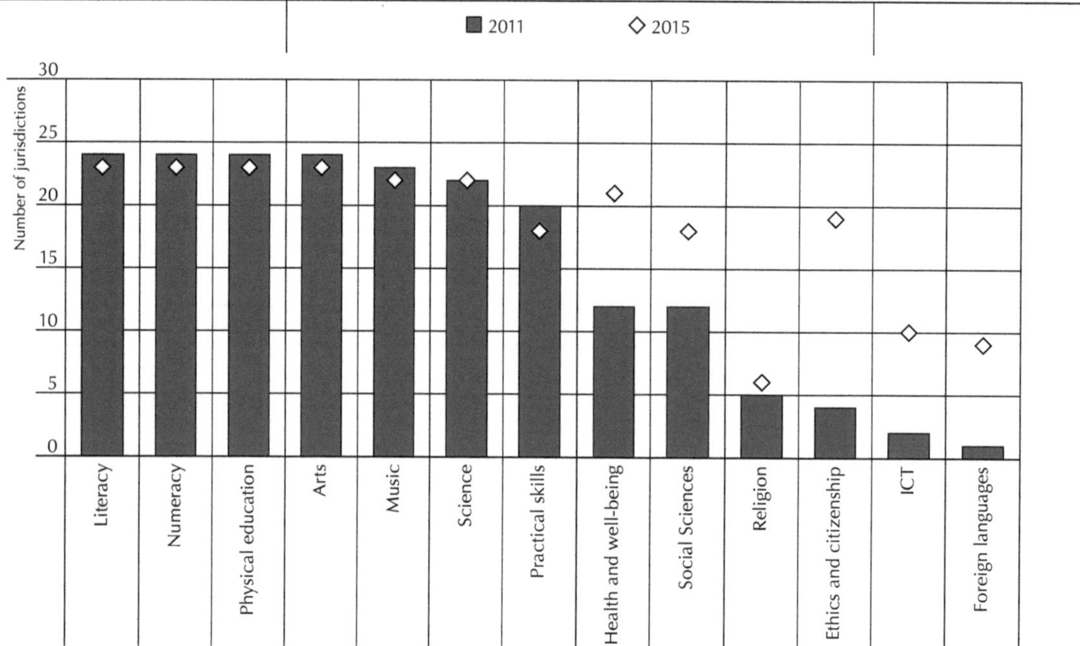

Note: Information on content areas of the curriculum is based on reports from 24 countries and jurisdictions with this information for both 2011 and in 2015. Jurisdictions are ranked in descending order of the number of content areas included in their early childhood education curriculum framework in 2011. Respondents could list more than one content category.

Belgium (Flemish Community): Data for 2015 reflect the content stated in the Developmental Objectives for 2.5- to 6-year-olds.

Luxembourg: Data for 2015 consist of the curriculum content in two parallel curricula in place (Bildungsrahmenplan für non-formale Bildung im Kindes und Jugendalter [0–12] and Plan d'Etudes de l'enseignement fondamental).

New Zealand: For 2015, curricula for the previous year of early childhood education and care are considered (The New Zealand Curriculum and Te Marautanga o Aotearoa).

Poland: In 2015, foreign languages were obligatory only for 5-year-olds.

Portugal: In 2015, kindergartens provided foreign language (last year of early childhood education and care).

Slovenia: In 2015, settings can organise foreign languages.

Source: OECD (2017), *Starting Strong V: Transitions from Early Childhood Education and Care to Primary Education,* Starting Strong, OECD Publishing, Paris, https://dx.doi.org/10.1787/9789264276253-en.

Box 3.1. Selected reforms of pre-primary curricula

Czech Republic: The Innovation of the Framework for Educational Programme of Pre-primary education was implemented in 2012.

Iceland: National curriculum guidelines for pre-primary were implemented in 2011.

Finland: Since 2015, participation in pre-primary education, starting at the age of 6, has been mandatory (one year). The objective is to improve children's learning prerequisites, thereby increasing educational equality. Implementation of the national core curriculum for pre-primary education, updated by the Finnish National Agency of Education, started in 2016, based on locally produced curricula. The new Act on Early Childhood Education and Care entered into force in September 2018, and the national core curriculum for early childhood education and care has been updated accordingly. The national core curricula for primary and secondary education have also been recently reformed.

Italy: The National Curriculum for early childhood education and care was revised in 2012 and included implementation of the European Framework of key competencies for lifelong learning.

Japan: Japan revised its National Curriculum of Day Care Centre Works in March 2008, clarifying the enhancement of staff quality and the expertise of all staff.

...

Korea: In 2012, Korea introduced the Nuri Curriculum, an integrated curriculum for early childhood kindergarten and nursery centres for 3-5 year-olds. It aims to promote the holistic development of children and establish overarching principles for becoming responsible citizens with financial support for tuition for all children, regardless of household income.

Mexico: Recent efforts to improve quality and coverage in early childhood education and care include the creation of a framework syllabus to help early childhood education and care institutions develop a curriculum that meets their specific needs.

New Zealand: The early childhood curriculum, Te Whāriki, has been updated to reflect changes in early learning contexts, theory and pedagogy since its original publication in 1996. Its original aspiration for children and bicultural framing have been retained and strengthened through the publication of two pathways – one for early childhood education services and one for kōhanga reo (an indigenous Māori curriculum model).

Norway: The 2017 revision of the Framework Plan for the Content and Tasks of Kindergartens emphasises co-operation, including with parents, and coherence in transitions from early childhood education and care to primary school.

Sweden: Improved curriculum for pre-primary education implemented in 2011.

Source: OECD (2017), *Starting Strong 2017: Key OECD Indicators on Early Childhood Education and Care* (OECD, 2017[49]); Shuey, E. et al., "Curriculum alignment and progression between early childhood education and care and primary school: A brief review and case studies", *OECD Education Working Papers* (Shuey et al., 2019[46]).

CONCLUSIONS

Both didactic and child-centred instruction may boost children's academic skills, and practitioners could combine different approaches; but there is some evidence suggesting the importance of the latter in supporting the development of socio-emotional skills, with positive longer-term outcomes.

The evidence suggests that a developmental approach provides a strong educational foundation for young children. An academic orientation on basic skills (for instance, concerning phonological awareness and letter knowledge) can be embedded in a curriculum of playful activities in small groups, including episodes of shared dialogical reading and talking with the early childhood education and care staff, to foster children's vocabulary, comprehension skills and world knowledge (Bus, Leseman and Neuman, 2012[24]; Dickinson et al., 2003[25]). This can also be considered "developmentally appropriate practice" and can be integrated in "intentional teaching" in early childhood education and care (Siraj-Blatchford, 2014[50]).

Teacher-directed approaches generally have clearly defined, specific aims and strategies, such as the development of academic skills. This can be an advantage for practitioners, since these are easier to apply. They may also make it easier to monitor children's development and conduct staff self-evaluations. On the other hand, giving children opportunities for autonomy may promote children's socio-emotional abilities, such as self-regulation and self-control. These are believed crucial for development and success as children progress through education, and policy documents and studies generally recommend combining both approaches and practices to stimulate early development.

While pedagogy is something that happens in staff-child interactions, policy can shape pedagogical environments, most notably through curriculum design and initial as well as continuing staff development. The OECD Starting Strong V report shows that in almost all countries, some form of curriculum or framework set at the national level is in place, and its prescribed learning areas and goals influence the pedagogical approaches and practices early childhood education and care providers espouse.

Public policy can also facilitate the transition from early childhood education and care to primary school, which is a major step for children. Well-managed transitions are important because they can support child well-being, ensure that the benefits of early childhood education and care endure, prepare children for school and for life, and improve equity in education outcomes. By integrating or aligning curricula across early childhood education and care, and primary school, governments can support continuity for young children while simultaneously promoting progress and setting strong foundations for later stages of education. At the same time, concerns about "schoolification" and age-appropriate practice need to be considered as curricula converge across levels.

Notes

1. The High/Scope curriculum uses a developmental-constructivist approach to early education, in which adults would engage children as active learners and children would have the opportunity to initiate much of their own activities (Schweinhart and Weikart, 1997[13]).

References

Barnett, W. et al. (2010), *The State of Preschool 2010: State Preschool Yearbook*, National Institute for Early Education Research, New Brunswick. [10]

Bell, N. (2017), *Update of Te Whāriki: Presentation to the 21st Meeting of OECD Network on ECEC*. [47]

Bertrand, J. (2007), "Preschool Programs: Effective Curriculum. Comments on Kagan and Kauerz and on Schweinhart", *Encyclopedia on Early Childhood Development*. [31]

Boyd, J. et al. (2005), *Promoting Children's Social and Emotional Development Through Preschool Education*, NIEER. [34]

Bredekamp, S. (1987), *Developmentally Appropriate Practice in Early Childhood Programs Serving Children from Birth Through Age 8*, NAEYC, Washington D.C. [7]

Burts, D. et al. (1992), "Observed activities and stress behaviors of children in developmentally appropriate and inappropriate kindergarten classrooms", *Early Childhood Research Quarterly*, Vol. 7/2, pp. 297-318, http://dx.doi.org/10.1016/0885-2006(92)90010-v. [14]

Bus, A., P. Leseman and S. Neuman (2012), "Methods for preventing early academic difficulties.", in *APA educational psychology handbook, Vol 3: Application to learning and teaching.*, American Psychological Association, Washington, http://dx.doi.org/10.1037/13275-021. [24]

Chazan-Cohen, R. et al. (2017), *Working toward a definition of infant/toddler curricula: Intentionally furthering the development of individual children within responsive relationships*, Office of Planning, Research and Evaluation. [32]

Copple, C. and S. Bredekamp (2009), *Developmentally Appropriate Practice in Early Childhood Programs Serving Children from Birth Through Age 8*, NAEYC, Washington D.C. [33]

DEEWR (2010), *Educators belonging, being and becoming: Educators' guide to the Early Years Learning Framework for Australia*, Department of Education, Employment, and Workplace Relations - Australia, http://files.acecqa.gov.au/files/National-Quality-Framework-Resources-Kit/educators_guide_to_the_early_years_learning_framework_for_australia.pdf (accessed on 13 December 2018). [41]

Dickinson, D. (2011), "Teachers' Language Practices and Academic Outcomes of Preschool Children", *Science*, Vol. 333/6045, pp. 964-967, http://dx.doi.org/10.1126/science.1204526. [19]

Dickinson, D. (2002), "Shifting Images of Developmentally Appropriate Practice as Seen Through Different Lenses", *Educational Researcher*, Vol. 31/1, pp. 26-32, http://dx.doi.org/10.3102/0013189x031001026. [8]

Dickinson, D. et al. (2003), "The comprehensive language approach to early literacy: The interrelationships among vocabulary, phonological sensitivity, and print knowledge among preschool-aged children.", *Journal of Educational Psychology*, Vol. 95/3, pp. 465-481, http://dx.doi.org/10.1037/0022-0663.95.3.465. [25]

Eurydice (2009), *Early Childhood Education and Care in Europe: Tackling Social and Cultural Inequalities*, Eurydice, Brussels. [11]

Frede, E. and D. Ackerman (2007), *Preschool curriculum decision-making: dimensions to consider, Preschool Policy Brief Issue 12*, National Institute for Early Education Research. [29]

Gersten, R., H. Walker and C. Darch (1988), "Relationship between Teachers' Effectiveness and Their Tolerance for Handicapped Students", *Exceptional Children*, Vol. 54/5, pp. 433-438, http://dx.doi.org/10.1177/001440298805400506. [20]

Goldberg, S. (2000), *Attachment and Development*, Arnold, London. [23]

Graue, E. et al. (2004), "More than teacher directed or child initiated: Preschool curriculum type, parent involvement, and children's outcomes in the child-parent centers.", *education policy analysis archives*, Vol. 12, p. 72, http://dx.doi.org/10.14507/epaa.v12n72.2004. [18]

Harris-Van Keuren, C. and D. Rodríguez Gómez (2013), *Early Childhood Learning Guidelines in Latin America and the Caribbean*, Inter-American Development Bank. [44]

Haskins, R. (1985), "Public School Aggression among Children with Varying Day-Care Experience", *Child Development*, Vol. 56/3, p. 689, http://dx.doi.org/10.2307/1129759. [15]

Huffman, L. and P. Speer (2000), "Academic performance among at-risk children: The role of developmentally appropriate practices", *Early Childhood Research Quarterly*, Vol. 15/2, pp. 167-184, http://dx.doi.org/10.1016/s0885-2006(00)00048-x. [4]

Jenkins, J. and G. Duncan (2017), *Do pre-kindergarten curricula matter?*, Brookings Institution and Duke University. [35]

Justice, L. et al. (2008), "Quality of language and literacy instruction in preschool classrooms serving at-risk pupils", *Early Childhood Research Quarterly*, Vol. 23/1, pp. 51-68, http://dx.doi.org/10.1016/j.ecresq.2007.09.004. [21]

Laevers, F. (2011), *Experiential Education: Making Care and Education More Effective Through Well-Being and Involvement*, Centre of Excellence for Early Childhood Development and Strategic Knowledeg Cluster on Early Child Development, Montreal. [12]

Lerkkanen, M. et al. (2012), "The role of teaching practices in the development of children's interest in reading and mathematics in kindergarten", *Contemporary Educational Psychology*, Vol. 37/4, pp. 266-279, http://dx.doi.org/10.1016/j.cedpsych.2011.03.004. [17]

Marcon, R. (2002), "Moving up the grades: Relationship between preschool model and later school success", *Early Childhood Research & Practice*, Vol. 4/1, pp. 1-24. [9]

Marcon, R. (1999), "Differential impact of preschool models on development and early learning of inner-city children: A three-cohort study.", *Developmental Psychology*, Vol. 35/2, pp. 358-375, http://dx.doi.org/10.1037/0012-1649.35.2.358. [22]

Marshall, C. (2017), "Montessori education: a review of the evidence base", *npj Science of Learning*, Vol. 2/1, http://dx.doi.org/10.1038/s41539-017-0012-7. [37]

McMullen, M. et al. (2005), "Comparing beliefs about appropriate practice among early childhood education and care professionals from the U.S., China, Taiwan, Korea and Turkey", *Early Childhood Research Quarterly*, Vol. 20/4, pp. 451-464, http://dx.doi.org/10.1016/j.ecresq.2005.10.005. [5]

Ministry of Education, Culture, Sports, Science and Technology, Japan (2017), *Course of Study for Kindergarten*, Ministry of Education, Culture, Sports, Science and Technology, Tokyo. [43]

Moser, T. et al. (2017), *European Framework of Quality and Wellbeing Indicators*, European Union CARE Project. [45]

NAEYC/NAECS-SDE (2003), "Early childhood curriculum, assessment, and program evaluation: Building an effective, accountable system in programs for children birth through age 8", *Position Statement*, https://www.naeyc.org/sites/default/files/globally-shared/downloads/PDFs/resources/position-statements/pscape.pdf (accessed on 13 December 2018). [39]

New Zealand Ministry of Education (2017), *Te Whāriki He whāriki mātauranga mō ngā mokopuna o Aotearoa Early Childhood Curriculum*, https://www.education.govt.nz/assets/Documents/Early-Childhood/Te-Whariki-Early-Childhood-Curriculum-ENG-Web.pdf. [40]

New Zealand Ministry of Education (2007), "The New Zealand Curriculum", http://nzcurriculum.tki.org.nz/The-New-Zealand-Curriculum (accessed on 13 December 2018). [48]

OECD (2018), *The Future of Education and Skills - Education 2030: The Future We Want*, OECD, Paris,, http://www.oecd.org/education/2030/E2030%20Position%20Paper%20(05.04.2018).pdf. [27]

OECD (2017), *Starting Strong 2017: Key OECD Indicators on Early Childhood Education and Care*, OECD Publishing, Paris, http://dx.doi.org/10.1787/9789264276116-3-en. [49]

OECD (2017), *Starting Strong V: Transitions from Early Childhood Education and Care to Primary Education*, Starting Strong, OECD Publishing, Paris, https://dx.doi.org/10.1787/9789264276253-en. [2]

OECD (2011), *Starting Strong III: A Quality Toolbox for Early Childhood Education and Care*, Starting Strong, OECD Publishing, Paris, https://dx.doi.org/10.1787/9789264123564-en. [30]

Ontario Government (2007), *Early Learning for Every Child Today: A framework for Ontario early childhood settings*, Ministry of Children and Youth Services, http://www.edu.gov.on.ca/childcare/oelf/continuum/continuum.pdf (accessed on 13 December 2018). [42]

Pramling-Samuelsson, I. and M. Fleer (2009), *Commonalities and distinctions accross countries*, Springer, New York. [6]

Schweinhart, L. and D. Weikart (1997), "The high/scope preschool curriculum comparison study through age 23", *Early Childhood Research Quarterly*, Vol. 12/2, pp. 117-143, http://dx.doi.org/10.1016/s0885-2006(97)90009-0. [13]

Shuey, E. et al. (2019), "Curriculum alignment and progression between early childhood education and care and primary school : A brief review and case studies", *OECD Education Working Papers*, No. 193, OECD Publishing, Paris, https://dx.doi.org/10.1787/d2821a65-en.   [46]

Sim, M. et al. (forthcoming), *Starting Strong Teaching and Learning International Survey 2018 Conceptual Framework*, OECD Publishing, Paris.   [3]

Siraj-Blatchford, I. (2014), *Early Childhood Education*, SAGE Publications, London.   [50]

Stipek, D. et al. (1998), "Good Beginnings: What difference does the program make in preparing young children for school?", *Journal of Applied Developmental Psychology*, Vol. 19/1, pp. 41-66, http://dx.doi.org/10.1016/s0193-3973(99)80027-6.   [26]

Stipek, D. et al. (1995), "Effects of Different Instructional Approaches on Young Children's Achievement and Motivation", *Child Development*, Vol. 66/1, pp. 209-223, http://dx.doi.org/10.1111/j.1467-8624.1995.tb00866.x.   [16]

Sylva, K., K. Ereky-Stevens and A. Aricescu (2015), *Overview of European ECEC curricula and curriculum template*, European Union CARE Project.   [38]

Sylva, K. et al. (2016), *Integrative Report on a culture-sensitive quality and curriculum framework*, European Union CARE Project.   [28]

Wall, S., I. Litjens and M. Taguma (2015), *Early Childhood Education and Care Pedagogy Review, England*, OECD, Paris, http://www.oecd.org/education/school/early-childhood-education-and-care-pedagogy-review-england.pdf.   [1]

Weiland, C. et al. (2018), "Preschool Curricula and Professional Development Features for Getting to High-Quality Implementation at Scale: A Comparative Review Across Five Trials", *AERA Open*, Vol. 4/1, p. 233285841875773, http://dx.doi.org/10.1177/2332858418757735.   [36]

CHILDREN, TECHNOLOGY AND TEACHING

Schools, and even early childhood educational institutions, are examining whether and how to incorporate information and communication technologies (ICT) into their learning environments. This chapter examines how these technologies can be used effectively for learning. It also discusses research on the impact of using these technologies – including television, video games and social media – on children's developing brains and bodies.

A note regarding Israel

The statistical data for Israel are supplied by and under the the responsibility of the relevant Israeli authorities. The use of such data by the OECD is without prejudice to the status of the Golan Heights, East Jerusalem and Israeli settlements in the West Bank under the terms of international law.

According to results from the 2015 cycle of the Programme for International Student Assessment (PISA), 95% of 15-year-old students, on average across OECD countries, have Internet access at home (OECD, 2017[1]). On a typical weekday, students spend more than two hours on line after school – an increase of 40 minutes since 2012 (OECD, 2017[1]). And children are "connected" in other places besides home. PISA 2012 data showed that, across OECD countries, 72% of students reported using computer technologies (desktops, laptops or tablets) at school (OECD, 2015[2]).

International trends are pointing to increases in use also among younger children (Hooft Graafland, 2018[3]). Some research suggests that preschoolers become familiar with digital devices before they are exposed to books (Brody, 2015[4]; Hopkins, Brookes and Green, 2013[5]).

Information and communication technology (ICT) can change the way children develop and learn. Not only schools, but also early childhood educational institutions are exploring ways to integrate ICT into learning environments. Some systems have already invested heavily in introducing ICT, while others have taken a more gradual approach. But the availability of ICT in educational institutions is only one aspect of this shift. Plans to expand access to technology in individual schools or educational institutions, entire districts or even whole countries need to take into account how these tools would be put to good use by both teachers and students in order to be effective.

Education systems need to re-evaluate their curricula and instructional systems, and teachers need to reassess their teaching styles, to ensure that ICT is used effectively to support learning and equip children with competencies that are important for the future. Linking the way children interact with ICT inside of school to the way they already use it outside of school could be the key to unlocking technology's potential for learning.

The rise in children's use of technology has also led to growing concern about how it affects children's brains and their socio-emotional, cognitive and physical development. Policy makers in various countries have already set guidelines for children's use of technology. This chapter draws on research from the OECD Centre for Educational Research and Innovation's 21st-Century Children project to summarise some of those guidelines and their rationale. It also reviews the literature on the effects of technology use on children's brain, and their cognitive, socio-emotional and physical development (Gottschalk, 2019[6]). The chapter also examines data from the OECD Programme for International Student Assessment (PISA) and the OECD Teaching and Learning International Survey (TALIS) related to the use of ICT at home and at school. The chapter ends with a look at the role of schools in supporting safe and responsible technology use (Hooft Graafland, 2018[3]), and a discussion of how education policy can address these issues.

TECHNOLOGY, LEARNING AND TEACHING

Technology can enable teachers and students to access specialised materials well beyond textbooks, in multiple formats and in ways that can bridge time and space. It can support new ways of teaching that focus on learners as active participants. There are good examples of technology enhancing experiential learning by supporting project- and enquiry-based teaching methods, facilitating hands-on activities and co-operative learning, and delivering formative real-time assessments. Teachers who "flip" their classrooms use class time for practice, group work and individual feedback, while asking students to watch or listen to lesson content at home. In doing so, they extend study time and individualise instruction. In flipped classrooms, technology is used as a means to reinforce pedagogical practice, but is not at the centre of the classroom experience (Bergmann and Sams, 2012[7]).

Technology can also compensate for space constraints. Virtual laboratories give students opportunities to design, conduct and learn from experiments, rather than just learning about them. Technology use in second-language instruction can give students access to native speakers who may not otherwise be available.

There are also interesting examples of technology supporting learning with interactive, non-linear courseware based on state-of-the-art instructional design, sophisticated software for experimentation and simulation, social media and educational games. These can be learning tools to develop 21st-century knowledge and skills. One teacher can now educate and inspire millions of learners and communicate their ideas to the whole world.

Perhaps the most distinguishing feature of technology is that it not only serves individual learners and educators, but it can build an ecosystem around learning that is predicated on collaboration. Technology can build communities of learners that make learning more social and more fun, recognising that collaboration enhances goal orientation, motivation, persistence and the development of effective learning strategies. Similarly, technology can build communities of teachers to share and enrich teaching resources and practices, and to collaborate on professional growth. It can help system leaders and governments develop and share best practice around curriculum design, policy and pedagogy.

That said, even where technology is used in classrooms, its impact on student performance is still mixed, at best. In 2015, PISA measured students' digital literacy, and the frequency and intensity with which students use computers at school.

Students who use computers moderately at school tend to have somewhat better learning outcomes than students who use computers rarely. But students who use computers frequently at school do a lot worse in most learning outcomes, even after accounting for socio-economic background and student demographics.

Figure 4.1
Time spent using the Internet and science performance
OECD average, 30 countries

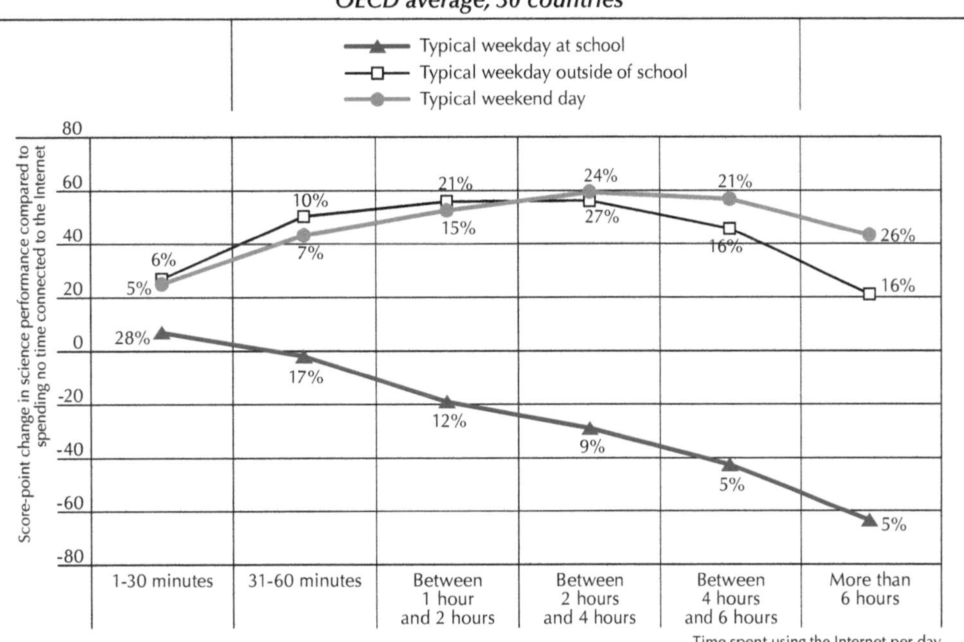

Notes: Results based on three separate linear regression models, one for each variable. Results after accounting for gender and socio-economic status. The reference category to which results are compared is "no time".
The percentage of students in each category is shown next to the marker. The remaining students answered "no time".
All coefficients are statistically significant.
Source: OECD, PISA 2015 Database.

Equally important, according to PISA 2015 data (Figure 4.1), technology used in the classroom still tends to emulate more traditional activities that could take place without digital devices. Browsing the Internet for schoolwork (48% of students across OECD countries reported doing this at least once a week) and chatting on line at school (the most rapidly growing activity, with a 24 percentage-point increase since 2012, on average across OECD countries) are activities that could otherwise be accomplished without technology, through more traditional research and discussion. Meanwhile, an average of just 15% of students reported doing simulations on computers at school – a technology-specific activity – at least once a week.

Hattie and Yates (2013[8]) explain that the successful use of computer-assisted instruction shares several characteristics with successful learning interventions that are not technology based: it extends study time and practice; it allows students to assume greater control over the learning situation (e.g. by individualising the pace with which new material is introduced); and it can support collaborative learning. In other words, the science of learning in a technology-rich world is similar to that in the analogue world. Learning demands time, and is most effective when it responds to a personal need or goal, and when it can be socially enhanced.

At the same time, teachers need to have a sense of ownership over technology. This means that technology should not only support teaching but also help teachers build on their pedagogical expertise (Paniagua and Istance, 2018[9]).

PISA data show that teachers' use of digital devices is related to the demands of the curriculum and to their own attitudes. In mathematics, teachers who ask students to work on real-world problems use computers most. But pedagogical knowledge and diversification of instruction are also important. Teachers who are most inclined towards, and better prepared for, student-oriented practices, such as group work, individualised learning, and project work, are more likely to use digital resources (OECD, 2015[2]).

Research also shows that participation in professional development activities that involve individual or collaborative research, or a network of teachers, is associated with a greater likelihood that a teacher will more frequently use ICT for students' work. In addition, teachers who report a positive disciplinary classroom climate are more likely to use ICT in their teaching. It is possible that a positive classroom climate is more conducive to the use of ICT (e.g. because of fewer disruptive students) or that the use of ICT helps to ameliorate classroom climate (e.g. because students enjoy interacting with technology). Teachers who hold constructivist beliefs about their job (i.e. those who see themselves as facilitators of students' own enquiry, or see thinking and reasoning as more important than specific curriculum content) are also more likely to use ICT and other active teaching techniques. This may be because ICT can enable students to pursue knowledge in more independent ways than traditional teaching, in line with the constructivist approach.

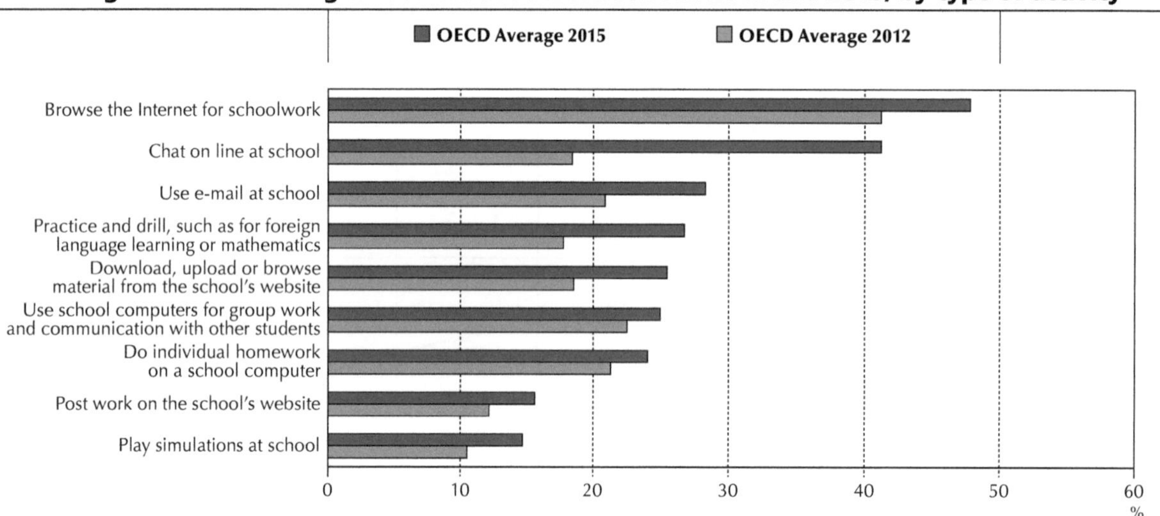

Figure 4.2

Change in the use of digital devices at school between 2012 and 2015, by type of activity

Source: OECD (2018), "Change in use of digital devices at school between 2012 and 2015, by type of activity", in *Teaching for the Future: Effective Classroom Practices To Transform Education*, OECD Publishing, Paris, https://doi.org/10.1787/9789264293243-graph5-en.

Box 4.1. Using technology to support enquiry-based science teaching

Information and communication technologies (ICTs) can provide teachers with the tools to support learning and can help students acquire the digital skills needed for the 21st century. However, the evidence of the effects of digital technologies in the classroom is not conclusive, especially when ICTs are combined with particular teaching practices (Bulman and Farlie, 2016[10]; Falck, Mang and Woessman, 2018[11]; Rodrigues and Biagi, 2017[12]).

In PISA 2015, students were asked to report on the availability and use of ICTs at school. Answers to the questions were then combined to construct two continuous composite indicators. These indicators were then examined in much the same way as the interaction between school climate and enquiry-based science teaching (EBST) was analysed. In addition to observed and unobserved school characteristics, the regressions included student profile and student-reported exposure to EBST, and the interaction between EBST and the two ICT indices.

The results of the regressions show the expected negative association between EBST and science performance. The interaction between EBST and availability of ICT resources in school is non-significant in almost all countries (except Bulgaria and Lithuania, where it is positive and significant, but weak). However, the interaction between EBST and the use of ICT resources is positive and significant in eight countries: Brazil, Bulgaria, the Dominican Republic, France, Lithuania, Poland, Slovenia and Uruguay. In all of these countries the association is weak, and varies between a 5 and 10 score-point change.

There is no clear and overwhelming evidence that EBST would be positively associated with science performance if ICTs are available and used at school to support this teaching practice. The results also suggest that in a few countries, using ICT resources to support learning is more important than just their availability.

Source: Mostafa, T., A. Echazarra and H. Guillou (2018), "The science of teaching science: An exploration of science teaching practices in PISA 2015", *OECD Education Working Papers*, http://dx.doi.org/10.1787/f5bd9e57-en

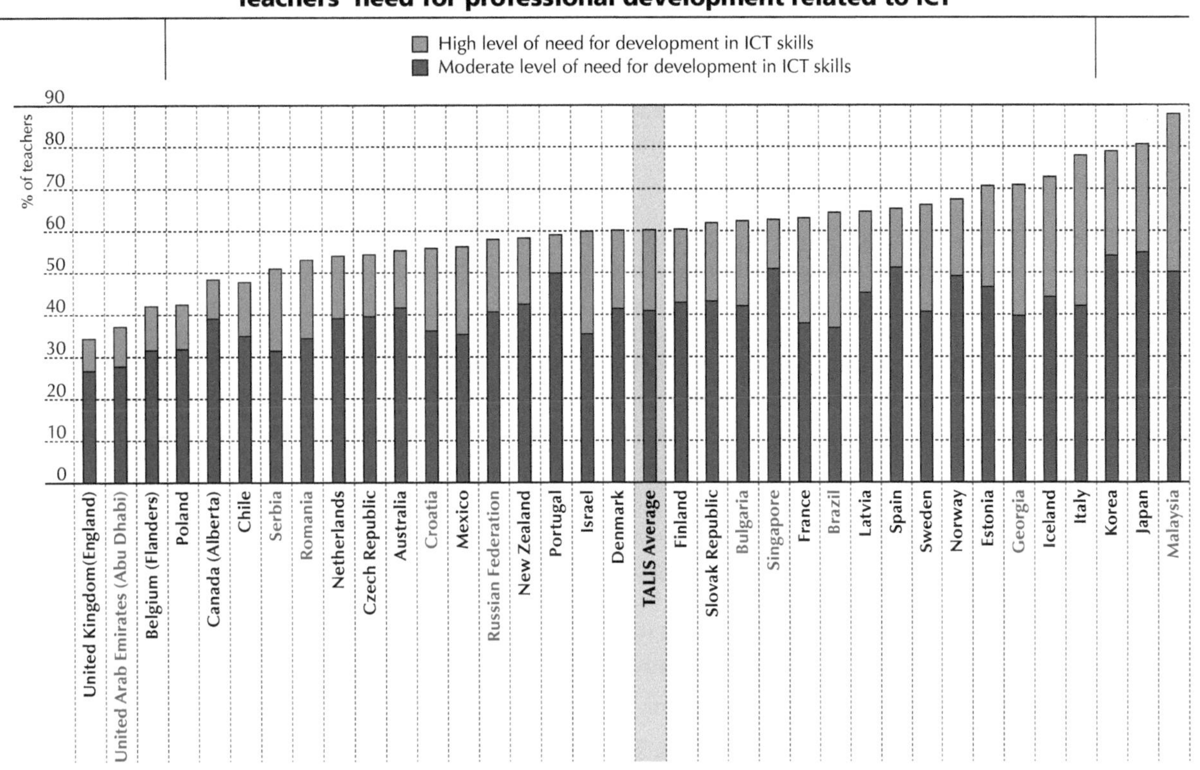

Figure 4.3

Teachers' need for professional development related to ICT

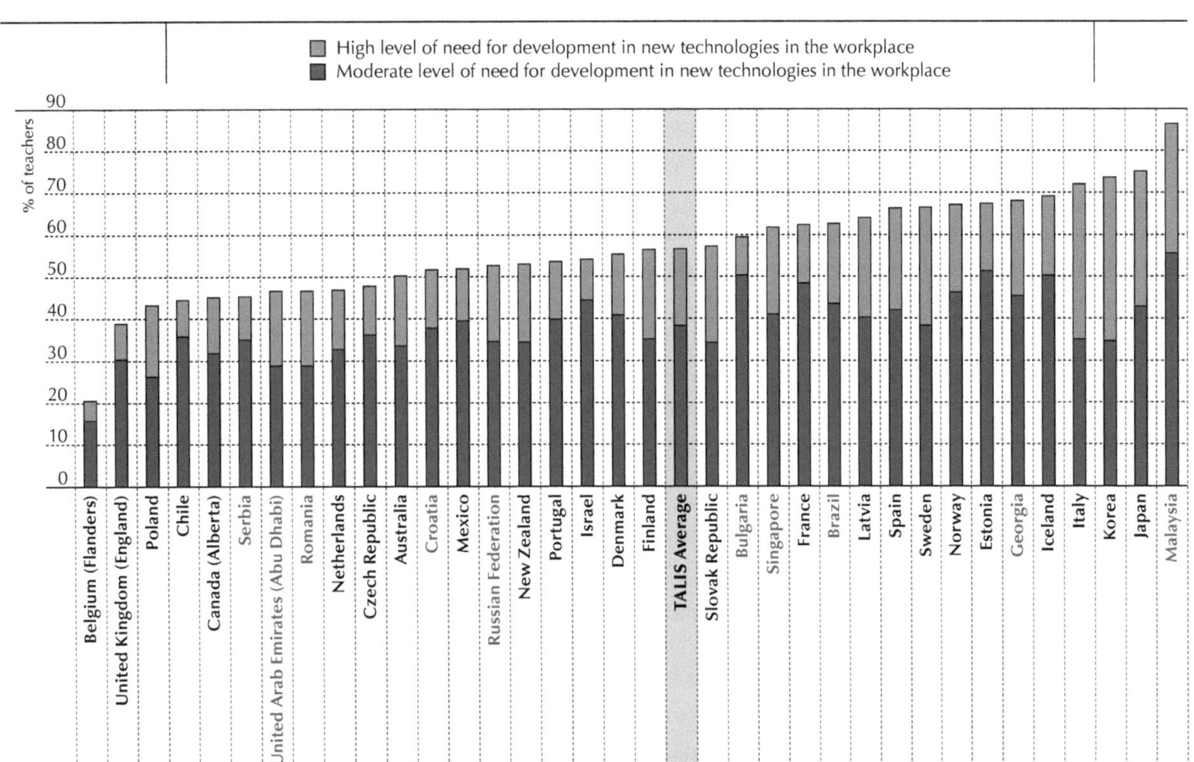

Source: OECD, TALIS 2013 database

Findings from the 2013 OECD Teaching and Learning International Survey (TALIS) show that about 60% of teachers report moderate or high development needs in ICT skills for teaching. This makes it the most commonly reported area for development after teaching students with special needs. In addition, over 56% of teachers report moderate or high development needs with the use of new technologies in the work place. This differs across countries, as Figure 4.2 illustrates. Around 55% of teachers who took part in TALIS reported participating in professional development activities relating to ICT skills for teaching; and about 40% of teachers reported participating in professional development courses in new technologies in the workplace. Teachers reported a positive impact on their teaching as a result of participating in these courses.

TECHNOLOGY, THE BRAIN, COGNITION AND WELL-BEING

Young people today are more "connected" than ever. In 2017, three out of four Internet users (aged 16 to 74) used the Internet daily or almost every day (OECD, 2019[13]). Digital engagement is generally higher among younger adults than older adults, although the differences today are less pronounced than ten years ago. In 2015, a typical 15-year-old from an OECD country had been using the Internet since the age of 10 and spent more than two hours every weekday on line after school, and more than three hours every weekend day (OECD, 2017[1]). PISA defines "extreme Internet users" as those who spend more than six hours per day on line; 26% of students in OECD countries fall into this category.

Young people have shown preferences for using the Internet for gaming, chatting and social networking (Durkee, 2012[14]). Today, children use mostly televisions and tablets, although the media landscape is becoming more complex. Children are watching less television than before, with an increase in the use of television services, such as Netflix and Amazon Prime, while YouTube is quickly becoming the viewing platform of choice, especially for 8-11 year-olds (Ofcom, 2019[15]). In addition to teenagers, there has been a significant increase in Internet usage among young children (aged 0-8) (Hooft Graafland, 2018[3]). In the United Kingdom, the most recent figures show that over 50% of children aged 3-4 go on line for at least 9 hours per week, and 82% of 5-7 year-olds spend at least 9.5 hours per week on line (Ofcom, 2019[15]).

These findings may be significant because of the "plasticity", or experience-dependent changes, of developing brains. The brain essentially changes in response to experiences, and childhood is a period of high brain plasticity. In the literature, the use of technology has been associated with both transient changes, i.e. changes in mood or arousal, and with long-term alterations in the brain or behaviour (Bavelier, Green and Dye, 2010[16]); see Gottschalk (2019[6]) for the full review.

The effects of technology may depend on factors such as the type of technology used and what it is used for (Bavelier, Green and Dye, 2010[16]). Children may use computers during class time, cell phones to keep in contact with friends, a tablet to do schoolwork in the evening, and then watch an hour of television with their families to unwind. This can add up to many hours over the course of the day. Therefore, understanding how and why technology is used, and the variety of devices children choose, can help determine whether limits to screen time are useful and how they should be set.

Many groups concerned with children's health, including governments and medical societies, advocate for partially or fully limiting screen time for children and adolescents. For example, the American Association of Pediatrics, a prominent international voice in child health, publishes guidelines for screen time for children age 0 to 18, the most recent of which were made available in 2016. These guidelines include a number of provisions, such as avoiding screens for children under 18 months (except for video chatting), and limiting to one hour per day high-quality programming for children up to age 5 (Table 4.1).

Many countries have published similar guidelines for parents and guardians suggesting limits to screen time and "best practices". Often, these are included as components of guidelines addressing the risks to children of a sedentary lifestyle, thus they reflect concerns about children's physical well-being more than their emotional or social well-being. Other general recommendations include turning off devices when not in use, switching off screens an hour before bed, and designating times (i.e. while having dinner or driving) and locations (i.e. the bedroom) as media-free. Table 4.1 outlines a small sample of screen-use guidelines released in different OECD countries, from governments or research institutes.

As can be seen in Table 4.1, the approaches taken by countries range from a "zero-tolerance approach" – the *carnet de santé* released by the French Ministry of Health and Solidarity, for example, suggests not even placing a child younger than three in a room where there is a television on (Ministère des Solidarités et de la Santé, 2018[17]) – to a more nuanced approach that focuses on types of screen time and how they affect family life.

A recent example of the latter approach is the 2019 Guidelines issued by the UK Royal College of Paediatrics and Child Health (Viner, Davie and Firth, 2019[18]). These guidelines were based on a comprehensive review of the evidence on the effects of screen time on children's physical and mental health. Given the lack of causal evidence linking screen time to negative child health, the guidelines focus on aspects of child well-being, such as online safety (i.e. from bullying, exploitation etc.) and access to inappropriate content. The main recommendation is that families negotiate screen time with children, based on the needs of the child and on which screens are in use and how they may or may not displace other health-related behaviours or social activities.

The guide poses four questions to be used by families to examine how they use screens. If families are satisfied with their responses, it is likely they are doing well regarding screen time. The questions are:

1. Is screen time in your household controlled?

2. Does screen use interfere with what your family wants to do?

3. Does screen use interfere with sleep?

4. Are you able to control snacking during screen time?

The guide finishes with a set of recommendations on how families can reduce screen time, if they feel the need. This includes protecting sleep, prioritising face-to-face interaction and being cognisant of parents' media use, as children tend to learn by example.

Table 4.1
Screen time recommendations in different countries

Country/institution	Infants/toddlers	Early childhood	School-age - adolescence	Other recommendations
AAP (United States)	None, except video chatting (under 18 mos). Only high quality programming (18-24 mos)	1 hour of high quality programming, co-view	Consistent limits on time and type	Turn off screens when not in use; ensure screen time doesn't displace other behaviours essential for health
Canada	None	<1 hour	<2 hours (CSEP only)	Limited sitting for extended periods (CSEP); Adults model healthy screen use (CPS)
-CSEP				
-Canadian Pediatric Society				
Australian Government Department of Health	None (under 12 mos); <1 hour (12-24 mos)	<1 hour	<2 hours (entertainment)	
New Zealand Ministry of Health	None	<1 hour	<2 hours (recreational)	Adapted from CSEP guidelines
German Federal Ministry of Health	None	30 minutes	1 hour (primary school) – 2 hours (adolescents)	Avoid as much as possible; avoid screen time completely for children under 2 including background television

Source: Gottschalk, F. (2019), "Impacts of technology use on children: Exploring literature on the brain, cognition and well-being", *OECD Education Working Papers*, No. 195, OECD Publishing, Paris, https://doi.org/10.1787/8296464e-en.

Although there is a great deal of media attention on this issue, it is important to separate fact from fiction when considering the impact of technology on children. According to a recent report, the weight given to screen time in both public and scientific discourse is probably not merited, based on the available data (Orben and Przylbylski, 2019[19]). It is essential, then, to review the available research. Furthermore, many children report that controlling media time is becoming more difficult, although the majority (aged 12-15) consider they have struck an appropriate balance (Ofcom, 2019[15]). The following sections summarise the full review found in Gottschalk (2019[6]).

A note on brain plasticity

The brain is plastic, and changes based on one's experiences. This plasticity is especially marked in the early years: research suggests rapid development and considerable plasticity in the brains of newborns through the first few years of life (Barkovich, 1988[20]). In addition, certain regions of the brain are more plastic than others, including the hippocampus, which is implicated in learning and memory (Bliss and Schoepfer, 2004[21]; Pastalkova, 2006[22]).

Childhood and adolescence are periods of rapid development and maturation. During the first three years of life, a child's brain may create over one million new connections per second[1] -- essential for the development of hearing, language and cognition (Center on the Developing Child, 2009[23]). These basic capacities create the foundation for higher-order functions, especially those formed in adolescence, as many neural networks underlying more complex activities, such as decision-making, mature during this time.

Structural and functional magnetic resonance imaging (fMRI)[2] studies have shown that these changes in function are accompanied by extensive structural alterations in the adolescent brain (Crone and Konjin, 2018[24]). Improvement of functions, such as attention and cognitive flexibility, for example, is likely a result of myelination and pruning (Luciana, 2013[25]; Paus, 2005[26]). Pruning refers to the selective elimination of synapses, which are initially overabundant in young brains. This process largely occurs throughout puberty and adolescence. The sensitive periods in early childhood and adolescence, when critical brain development and reorganisation occur, can be strongly influenced by experiences and environmental factors that can affect future functioning (Irwin, Siddiqi and Hertzman, 2007[27]; Petanjek, 2011[28]).

These sensitive periods used to be known as "critical periods", as it was believed that they were windows of opportunity in brain development that, if missed, would lead to the loss or underdevelopment of critical abilities. However, research has demonstrated that development of language and visual processes, for example, once thought to occur only during the "critical periods" of early childhood, can occur outside of this window (Fuhrmann, Knoll and Blakemore, 2015[29]).

While it underlies learning, neuroplasticity is not an inherently good or bad thing. Outcomes vary, depending on the magnitude and location of changes taking place.

Measuring these changes and activation patterns can be difficult. For example, fMRI allows for the detection of brain activity as shown through changes in local cerebral blood flow and from changes in oxygenation concentration (Glover, 2011[30]). However, it does not clarify the neural mechanisms underlying certain functions (i.e. cognitive or behavioural functions) (Logothetis, 2008[31]). Brain imaging can give some insight into brain structure and activation patterns, but functional relevance is difficult to infer, and this type of research remains exploratory.

IMPACT OF TELEVISION ON CHILDREN: COGNITION AND WELL-BEING

There is a relatively large body of literature exploring television and children, partly because television has been around for a long time. Researchers have explored the implications on verbal abilities, as well as cognitive, physical and emotional development. However, the quantity of research in this field outpaces the quality; many studies report very small effect sizes, are correlational in nature (they are unable to show causality), and there is much contradicting "evidence" presented even when analysing the same datasets. Thus, results in this domain must be interpreted with caution. This section provides an overview of some of the literature regarding television viewing and child outcomes, and some of its limitations.

Some research has linked viewing television for longer periods of time during childhood with attention problems in adolescence (Landhuis, 2007[32]), and suggests there may be modest adverse effects of watching television before the age of three on cognitive outcomes later in childhood (Zimmerman and Christakis, 2005[33]). However the research in this domain tends to be contradictory, and there is no clear impact (either positive or negative) of moderate television viewing (Foster and Watkins, 2010[34]). Some research has found no association with outcomes such as attention problems/hyperactivity, emotional symptoms, relationship problems and prosocial behaviour (behaviour intended to help other people, or benefit society generally), or with these outcomes and playing electronic games (Parkes, 2013[35]).

Results implicating television watching in the socio-emotional development of infants have also been inconsistent (Haughton, Aiken and Cheevers, 2015[36]). However, some of the literature points to more positive associations between watching television (in this case, educational programming) and children's development, suggesting it may promote literacy, mathematics, problem-solving and science skills, and prosocial behaviour in preschool-aged children (see Evans Schmidt and Anderson, (2009[37]).

Some scholars cite an opportunity cost associated with time spent watching television rather than engaging in more "educational" activities. For example, time spent playing attention-training games versus watching popular children's videos may contribute to improvements in executive attention and intelligence (Rueda, M. et al, 2005[38]).

Analyses of how children's brains react to television are more scarce than those concerning cognitive or behavioural outcomes, and causality remains difficult to ascertain. Despite these limitations, some results indicate that children who frequently watch TV are likely to engage less in physical activity, which, in turn, may have an impact on the volume of certain brain regions (Takeuchi et al., 2013[39]). This research is limited, however, by its small samples; therefore it is not clear whether TV viewing directly causes the outcomes measured, and whether the results are generalisable. In addition, the functional relevance of volumetric changes in different brain regions is not always clear.

In sum, the effects of television viewing on children are not clear. If time spent watching television is time away from other activities, particularly those that are beneficial for children's physical well-being, then there could be cause for concern. However, the evidence is mixed and there is no clear proof that moderate television watching displaces other activities essential for well-being or development.

On co-viewing

The benefits of "co-viewing" (i.e. when parents watch videos with children) are supported by a number of studies (see Gottschalk, (2019[6]), for an overview). While co-viewing with their parents or guardians, infants may pay more attention and potentially increase their ability to learn from video content (Barr et al., 2008[40]). This "scaffolding" suggests that parents pose questions, and give descriptions and labels during viewing (Barr et al., 2008[40]). But the extent of the cognitive outcomes associated with this practice is unclear.

Other cross-sectional research suggests that television watching, reading and physical activity when done with a caregiver every day is associated with higher linguistic and/or cognitive development than for children who engage in these activities only once or twice per week (Lee, Spence and Carson, 2017[41]). One conclusion here might be that, independent of the content of the activity, simply engaging in behaviours with a caregiver may be beneficial for child development (Lee, Spence and Carson, 2017[41]).

Another note about co-viewing, and parental mediation of screen content more generally, is that there is a deepening divide between socio-economically advantaged and disadvantaged families. Children whose parents are able to spend time both curating and mentoring screen time may reap more benefits than those in families with less financial resources and with parents who are less involved in daily activities (Canadian Paediatric Society, Digital Health Task Force, Ottawa, Ontario, 2017[42]). The equity dimension of television viewing has broader implications, especially if there is a relationship between cognitive outcomes and time spent watching television: children from disadvantaged backgrounds or with low-educated mothers tend to watch more television than children from advantaged backgrounds (Certain and Kahn, 2002[43]; Rideout and Hamel, 2006[44]).

"High-quality" programming: The quality vs. quantity debate

Not all television is created equal. While there is much content with little purpose beyond entertainment, educational programming does exist. There is not much research exploring brain-based outcomes of viewing educational television; but there is a relatively large body of research supporting the positive effects of educational programming on cognitive development in preschool-aged children (Anderson and Subrahmanyam, 2017[45]).

Some research suggests greater levels of school readiness (Anderson, 1998[46]; Anderson, D. et al, 2001[47]; Schmidt and Anderson, 2007[48]) and superior language development (Linebarger and Vaala, 2010[49]; Linebarger and Walker, 2005[50]; Linebarger and Piotrowski, 2009[51]) among preschoolers who watched Sesame Street regularly. Other "educational" shows have also been linked to better language use and vocabulary development (Linebarger and Walker, 2005[50]).

Engaging with educational content may be especially beneficial for children from disadvantaged and middle-class families, not only for their vocabulary, but also for their performance in reading and mathematics tests, and overall school readiness (Wright et al., 2001[52]). The benefits of engaging with this type of content may also last beyond early childhood. For example, some research has noted a positive relationship between viewing educational/informative television programmes during preschool years and both high school achievement and time spent reading books for leisure (Anderson, D. et al, 2001[47]).

A systematic review of the literature exploring the association between television viewing and outcomes such as academic performance, language and play, finds that the relationship between television and children's development is complex, and highlights the potential importance of individual characteristics, including social context and family factors. The review suggests that watching high-quality content is associated with academic skills and is predictive of future academic performance, whereas watching television during infancy may be detrimental to play and language development (Kostyrka-Allchorne, Cooper and Simpson, 2017[53]). It is unclear whether some of these interactions are long-lasting. In general, the nature of this type of research does not allow for causal inferences.

Despite these results, it is important to keep in mind the notion of the "video deficit", which posits that infants and toddlers do not learn as well from materials presented via video as they do from live sources (Anderson and Pempek, 2005[54]).

This video deficit may also affect language learning in infants during their first year of life, as viewing television before the age of two has some negative associations with language development and executive functions (Anderson and Subrahmanyam, 2017[45]). Live exposure, versus audio or video exposure, to foreign languages seems to have a stronger impact on the capacity to discern differences in phonetic units in languages (Kuhl, Tsao and Liu, 2003[55]).

In sum, there may be some benefits associated with engaging with child-tailored, educational content in terms of improved verbal abilities, cognitive development and neural maturity in children. However, the research also suggests that children learn better from live sources than from videos. This could also have implications for children from disadvantaged

households or with working parents who have less time to spend with them. Watching television can perhaps be incorporated into a schedule filled with other health- and development-promoting habits, even for infants and young children. Limiting television viewing for children who do not exhibit problematic tendencies is perhaps unnecessary. But the evidence can be contradictory, and it is difficult to distinguish clear associations between screen-time habits and cognitive outcomes.

EFFECTS OF VIDEO GAMES ON THE BRAIN AND EXECUTIVE FUNCTIONS

The literature on video gaming and children is much more recent than that on television; as a result it is also less conclusive. The majority of the research focuses on negative rather than positive outcomes (Granic, Lobel and Engels, 2014[56]), thereby providing a somewhat skewed view on the potential impact of video games on children. Providing a coherent and balanced view is important, especially as online gaming is becoming increasingly popular: three out of four of the 5-15 year-olds in the United Kingdom who play games do so on line (Ofcom, 2019[15]).

Positive findings include improved decision making (The IMAGEN Consortium, 2011[57]) and better procedural learning, i.e. acquiring new skills via practice (Pujol et al., 2016[58]). Action video games in particular (i.e. as distinguished from non-action video games by their speed, unpredictable stimuli and high sensory-motor load) have been linked to better reading outcomes for dyslexic children as well (Franceschini et al., 2017[59]). One study showed that even modest amounts of gaming have been associated with faster motor-response times (Pujol et al., 2016[58]).

Each of these individual findings would need to be supported with a more critical mass of evidence in order to be used to guide policy making; and these results would need to be considered in light of the concerns associated with excessive gaming. These concerns are widespread: "Internet Gaming Disorder" was recently included in the Appendix of the Diagnostic and Statistical Manual of Mental Disorders-V and as "Gaming disorder" in the draft of the 11th revision of the World Health Organization's International Classification of Diseases. However, formal classification of these ideas as "disorders" is contentious in the scientific community (Turel et al., 2014[61]), especially as research in this domain is not robust enough to liken "Internet addiction" or "gaming addiction" to substance addictions (Weinstein and Lejoyeux, 2015[62]). In line with multiple research findings, terms such as "excessive Internet use" are suggested in order to avoid using medical classification or terminology (Smahel, 2012[63]; Kardfelt Winther, 2017[64]) to describe children's online habits (OECD, 2017[1]; OECD, 2018[65]).

Parents and educators often worry about the impact of gaming on educational attainment; but as with "educational television", "educational gaming" might have positive effects on children. In general, there is a lack of strong evidence supporting the notion that video gaming affects education outcomes.

The literature in this domain is contradictory, and one of the biggest research challenges is accurately determining the amount of time spent gaming. This field, would benefit from more randomised-controlled trials, larger sample sizes, and more consistently reproducible findings. At present, all that can be said with certainty is that playing video games may have both positive and negative impacts on children, in part due to moderate versus more extreme use.

21ST-CENTURY CHILDREN AND SOCIAL MEDIA

Adolescents (and, to a lesser extent, children) in the 21st century use technology to interact with their peers. Since 1997, over 10 000 published journal articles have used the term "social media", with experts in fields such as psychology, economics and sociology incorporating this topic into their research agendas (Meshi, Tamir and Heekeren, 2015[66]). There is a good reason for this: recent estimates suggest that over 90% of young people use social media both day and night (Duggan and Smith, 2014[67]).

Texting is a dominant form of daily communication among adolescents, as are media such as instant messaging, social-media platforms and video chatting (Lenhart, 2015[68]). There is evidence to suggest that children's social relationships can be stimulated through digital technology and that moderate online communication has a positive relationship with the quality of friendship and social capital (for a review, see Kardefelt-Winther, (2017[64]).

There are differences in how young people use social media compared with older populations. As shown in Figure 4.3., in 2018, 35% of teenagers surveyed by the Pew Research Center in the United States reported that they use Snapchat most often, unlike their elders, who tend to favour Facebook (Pew Research Center, 2018[69]).

Despite the proliferation of research exploring social media use and the huge numbers of children subscribing to these platforms, empirical research on the impact of social media on the brain is scarce. In 2015, only seven published articles explored neurosciences and social media (Meshi, Tamir and Heekeren, 2015[66]). Furthermore, many studies focus on Facebook use; the literature exploring other social media used by 21st-century children, such as Snapchat and Instagram, is thin.

Figure 4.4

Change between 2015 and 2018 in use of social media platforms among US teenagers

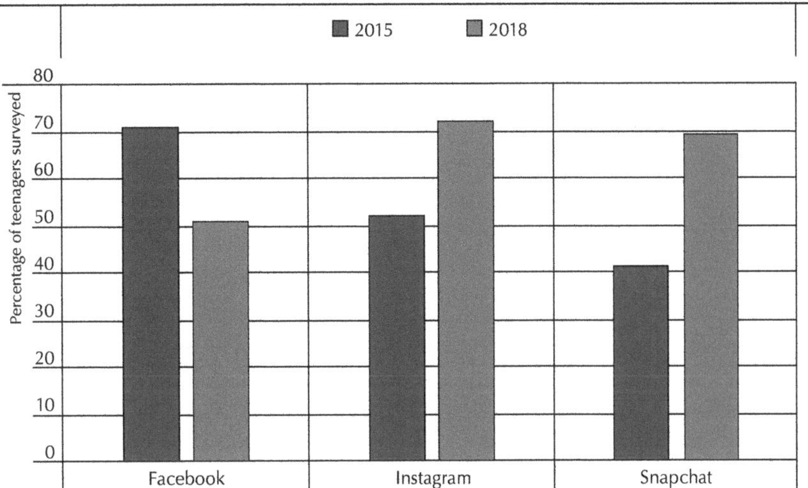

Source: Gottschalk, F. (2019), "Impacts of technology use on children: Exploring literature on the brain, cognition and well-being", *OECD Education Working Papers*, No. 195, OECD Publishing, Paris, https://doi.org/10.1787/8296464e-en.

Box 4.2. The Internet and interpersonal skills and well-being

What is the effect of electronic communication on children's interpersonal skills and well-being? Research has shifted over the past decades:

- The displacement theory argues that online interaction replaces face-to-face interaction, which in turn leads to reduced social involvement and psychological well-being among children who use the Internet (Kraut, R. et al, 1998[73]). Although this theory received early support, more recent studies that highlight the positive effects of the Internet on children's social capital have criticised the theory as simplistic.

- The "rich get richer" theory states that children with more social skills and networks will benefit more from online communication than those without (Kraut, R. et al, 1998[73]; UNICEF, 2017[74]).

- The social compensation hypothesis predicts that online communication benefits socially anxious and lonely children most as the Internet reduces social boundaries, thus facilitating making friends on line (Bonetti, Campbell and Gilmore, 2010[75]). Lonely teens are also more likely to use social networks to make new friends rather than maintaining existing friendships.

- Finally, the stimulation hypothesis suggests that the impact of children's online behaviour is mostly positive for all children and, in particular, that communication with existing friends is improved (UNICEF, 2017[74]; Valkenburg and Peter, 2007[76]; Miller and Morris, 2016[77]). A recent study, conducted among children in the United States, found a positive relation between children's computer use and the number of friends they communicated with off line (Fairlie and Kalil, 2017[78]). Another study, using Health Behaviour in School-aged Children (HBSC) data across nine countries, showed that 11-15 year-olds who communicated more through electronic media reported greater life satisfaction. However, above a certain threshold this relationship became negative (Boniel-Nissim et al., 2014[79]).

Although the displacement theory no longer receives much support, there is no consensus among researchers. More long-term research is needed that also takes into account the type of electronic communication or social network.

Source: (Hooft Graafland, 2018[3]), "New technologies and 21st-century children: Recent trends and outcomes, *OECD Education Working Papers*, No. 179, OECD Publishing, Paris, https://doi.org/10.1787/e071a505-en.

In addition, most research focuses on adults, not children or young people. There is some research to suggest that the use of social media, especially at night, may be linked to poor sleep quality. It also may be linked to levels of anxiety and depression, although the direction of causality is not clear and the relationships can be weak. In one particular study, for example, associations were stronger between poor sleep quality and anxiety/depression, than between media use and anxiety/depression) (Woods and Scott, 2016[70]).

Young people tend to maintain social media portfolios, consisting of accounts on different platforms, to share photos, updates and connect with peers. Adolescents, in particular, value the opinions of their peers, and the simple act of peers "liking" a recently published photo serves as a "quantifiable social endorsement" (Sherman et al., 2016[71]). More "popular" photos (i.e. those with more "likes") can elicit different responses from young people than less popular ones. For example, they tend to garner more likes even when showing risky behaviours, such as smoking marijuana and drinking alcohol, and certain brain regions show higher activity levels when viewing these posts, such as those associated with social memories, cognition and imitation, and the visual cortex (Sherman et al., 2016[70]).

"Facebook addiction", excessive social media use and risky behaviours

"Facebook addiction" and other classifications of excessive media use have gained traction in policy and research spheres. However, as with "gaming addiction" and Internet Gaming Disorder, these classifications are not universally recognised.

Even though more children are using social media than ever before, research on the effects of that activity on developing brains is still in its infancy. The use of social media has been connected to facial recognition and memory, which could prove beneficial in establishing and maintaining strong social networks both on line and off, in adolescence and later in life. However, directional causality cannot be inferred, and often the functional relevance of certain brain phenomena is unclear.

As this is a fast-moving area, the importance of using rigorous research is more necessary than ever (OECD, 2018[65]). At present, there appears to be a disconnect between the available evidence, media and public perception. Claims that "smartphones have ruined a generation" and "new technology 're-wires' children's brains" are largely unfounded: changes in the brain (i.e. plasticity) are normal developmental processes in childhood and adolescence, and any major "rewiring" as a result of technology use is unlikely (Kardfelt-Winther, 2017[64]). However, it is clear that this is an area of study that will need constant updating and refinement as technology evolves.

IMPLICATIONS FOR PHYSICAL HEALTH

Using ICTs is associated with various health-related outcomes and behaviours, including sleep patterns, posture and lifestyle. The following sections assess some of the potential risks and benefits of technology use on developing bodies [for the full review, see (Gottschalk, 2019[6])].

Sleep

The circadian rhythm is dependent on an internal clock. While not the only modulating factor of the circadian rhythm, light plays a major role in adjusting and synchronising these clocks (Touitou, Touitou and Reinberg, 2016[80]). Light that emits short wavelengths, such as blue and blue-green light, versus the longer wavelengths of orange or red light, has more of an effect on circadian rhythms (Brainard and Hanifin, 2002[81]; Thapan, Arendt and Skene, 2001[82]). Many devices today emit short-wavelength or blue light. This includes computers, cell phones and tablets, which over time have evolved to have larger and brighter screens.

Dosage (i.e. time spent engaging with devices) and age might affect melatonin production, important for signalling the onset of sleep. Adolescents and children might be more sensitive to light than adults, and more time using a device has been associated with a greater reduction in melatonin (Figueiro and Overington, 2016[83]). A systematic review of the literature uncovered 67 studies from 1999 to 2014 examining sleep patterns among school-aged children and adolescents. Some 90% of the studies found adverse associations between screen time and sleep outcomes, such as delayed timing and shortened duration of sleep (Hale and Guan, 2015[84]). However, association, or correlation, does not imply causality. Furthermore, there are often measurement errors regarding the amount of screen time and sleep time (Hale and Guan, 2015[84]). For example, teenagers are likely to over-report sleep time; and there is little research to validate assessments of adolescents' time in front of a screen using self-reported and parent-reported measures (Hale and Guan, 2015[84]).

In addition, different types of media use at bedtime might have different implications for sleep. For example, in a cross-sectional study of 11-13 year-olds in the United Kingdom, difficulty falling asleep was most associated with activities such as using mobile phones and listening to music, whereas reduction in weekday sleep duration was linked to visiting social media sites and using a computer for studying (Arora et al., 2014[85]). Some of these results were hypothesised to be due to a combination of delayed melatonin release, resulting from exposure to light emission, as well as mental excitation (Arora et al., 2014[85]). The findings specifically concerning computer use for studying and its impact on sleep are particularly

noteworthy, as over 50% of adolescents across OECD countries reported browsing the Internet for schoolwork outside of school at least once per week, according to PISA 2012 data (OECD, 2015[2]).

Establishing limits on when children and adolescents use technology (i.e. not in the hours immediately preceding bedtime), or providing children with protective equipment, such as blue light-blocking glasses, may help prevent sleep disruptions. Evidence suggests that these glasses are effective in mitigating melatonin suppression in teenagers (van der Lely et al., 2015[86]), so using them for late-night studying or scrolling through social media feeds before bedtime might be warranted. More research is needed to identify whether activating features on mobile devices, such "night shift" or "night mode", are effective in avoiding disruption of melatonin production. These steps could be incorporated into good sleep-hygiene practices, which include avoiding excess (or any) caffeine, engaging in regular exercise, maintaining a regular sleep schedule and eliminating noise from the sleeping environment (Stepanski and Wyatt, 2003[87]).

Stress

When faced with a stressor, threat or a challenge, the human body responds by secreting glucocorticoids, such as cortisol, that help prepare the body to react (i.e. activating the "fight or flight" response) (Juster, McEwen and Lupien, 2010[88]; Afifi et al., 2018[89]). In healthy people, the levels of cortisol follow a cyclic pattern and generally peak after waking, then drop steeply at various times in the day, with the lowest point before bedtime (Afifi et al., 2018[89]). Changes in this pattern or chronically high or low levels of cortisol can have negative effects on human physiology and psychological outcomes (Davidson and Irwin, 1999[90]; Damasio, 2000[91]).

Long periods of ICT use (i.e. three hours or more per day) and the type of media used might affect the cortisol response in children (Wallenius et al., 2010[92]). In one study looking at Facebook use by 12-17 year-olds (n=88), cortisol profiles were associated with Facebook network size and Facebook peer interactions. Further research suggests that the adolescents who engage more with general media, use their phones more and have larger networks on Facebook may show, upon waking, greater rises in cortisol (associated with poor mental and physical health) and rates of interleukin-6 (an inflammatory marker whose overproduction is associated with poor health) (Afifi et al., 2018[89]). Experimental and/or longitudinal work in this field can determine whether media use causes this biological response, or whether the response is a stimulator for media use.

Stress can be measured through biological markers, including cortisol, and also through subjective measures, such as respondents' reports of perceived stress. In response to stressful events, children may consume media to manage stress or mood through entertainment. Some studies show that playing games can help reduce physical stress temporarily and improve one's mood (Russoniello, O'Brien and Parks, 2009[137]). Social support offered in online and offline forums can help buffer the effects of stressful life events (Leung, 2007[93]).

Overeating, sedentary lifestyles and obesity

Over recent decades, increases in television watching and using the computer have raised concerns about obesity in children. Certain habits associated with screen time have been linked with body mass, especially in children. Eating while watching television, for example, has been associated with an increase in energy intake (i.e. more calories or food eaten) because it can delay normal mealtime satiation (i.e. the feeling of fullness), and because it can obscure signals of satiety from foods that had been previously consumed (i.e. children do not stop eating, even though they are already full) (Bellissimo et al., 2007[94]).

Further links with obesity and screen time tend to be less linear. For example, some literature points to the notion of a "displacement effect", whereby time spent using technology causes harm proportional to exposure, and detracts from other potentially more "valuable" activities (Neuman, 1988[95]). However, a recent review of the literature suggests that reducing screen time may not motivate adolescents and children to engage more in physical activity (Kardfelt-Winther, 2017[64]); see also Box 4.2); other research has shown that screen-based, sedentary behaviour and leisure-time physical activity are independent of one another (Gebremariam et al., 2013[96]). Television watching may displace other activities, such as reading, but the overall evidence of the negative impact of displacement is relatively weak (Evans Schmidt and Anderson, 2009[37]).

In any case, displacement effects can differ based on the extent of screen time and the activities being displaced. For example, heavy Internet use may interfere with participation in clubs and sports, whereas moderate use has been shown to encourage participation (Romer, Bagdasarov and More, 2013[96]). This is a relatively consistent finding across the research: moderate Internet use, and shared media experiences, allow young people to build rapport with their peers (Romer, Bagdasarov and More, 2013[98]; Romer, Jamieson and Pasek, 2009[99]; Pasek et al., 2006[100]).

Activity, energy and co-ordination

With developments in technology, there has been a shift in video games from being sedentary and controller-based to requiring players to engage in physical movements in order to interact with the screen-based game (Norris, Hamer and Stamatakis, 2016[101])). Augmented reality games, or those that involve geo-tracking (or in the case of Pokémon GO, a game that uses both) are also becoming increasingly popular; some argue that they promote movement.

But the evidence is mixed. A systematic review of the literature on using active video games as effective health interventions in schools found that the quality of the research was not high enough, and recommended randomised controlled trials with larger samples (Norris, Hamer and Stamatakis, 2016[101]). In contrast, a meta-analysis including 35 articles on active video games concluded that these games can be a good alternative to sedentary behaviour, although they are not replacements for more traditional sports and physical activity for children and adolescents. Results from this meta-analysis, however, ranged from null to moderate effect sizes (Gao et al., 2015[102]).

Technology might also be used to enhance the development of physical skills. For example, using applications on an iPad that require motor skills has been associated with improvements in motor co-ordination (Axford, Joosten and Harris, 2018[103]). With the emergence of skill-training applications and active video games, such as Wii Sports and Dance Dance Revolution, recommendations of screen use for children and adolescents may need to be re-evaluated. However, simply providing children with access to active video games is unlikely to prompt spontaneous engagement in more physical activity and may not benefit public health (Baranowski et al., 2012[104]). More research in this field is needed to ascertain whether and how active video games can be used to boost children's activity and fitness.

Musculoskeletal discomfort and posture

There are other physiological implications associated technology use. Musculoskeletal discomfort associated with children's computer use has been noted in a number of studies (Jacobs and Baker, 2002[105]); Woo, White and Lai, 2016[144]), as have the risks to posture associated with the use of computers and tablets. Certain conditions, including asymmetrical and sustained positions of the lower extremities, and holding a posture for more than one minute might contribute to the discomfort, as could using a tablet rather than a laptop, which might result in more sustained neck flexion (Ciccarelli, 2015[106]). More recent evidence also suggests an increase in adverse neck symptoms related to television, phone and tablet use, and adverse visual symptoms related to more frequent use of cell phones and tablets (Straker, 2017[107]).

Parents, educators and young people should all be aware of how to identify risks to their posture (Ciccarelli, 2015[106]). Physically changing where in the home or school children use devices can help vary the postures used. Adults can help children understand that changes in posture and taking active breaks to include stretching and movement can be beneficial (Harris, 2015[108]). Teacher-training programmes for pre- and in-service teachers could also include modules on how teachers and students can counter the adverse physical effects of sustained or static positions when using computers – or simply when sitting in class (Murphy, Buckle and Stubbs, 2004[109]).

SAFE AND RESPONSIBLE INTERNET USE: THE ROLE OF SCHOOLS

Schools play a key role in supporting safe and responsible Internet use. The challenge for schools lies in their ability to reduce the negative uses of the Internet and digital devices while maintaining their contributions to teaching, learning and social connection (Kaveri Subrahmanyam and Patricia Greenfield, 2008[110]). In order to do this, children should be taught how to manage rather than avoid risks online (Middaugh, Clark and Ballard, 2017[111]). This section discusses the best approaches used by schools to support students in their digital use (for the full discussion, see (Hooft Graafland, 2018[3]).

School organisation and policies

A whole-school approach, where teachers and support staff are able to recognise, respond and resolve online safety issues, is found to be effective in protecting and supporting students in their use of technology (Ofsted, 2014[112]). It is thus essential to train teachers and support staff in online risks and their implications. Training should be provided on a regular basis, as digital technology is changing rapidly and it is important for teachers to stay up-to-date with new developments. Parents and students can also get involved to strengthen the school's capacity to deal with online safety issues.

In addition to a whole-school approach, online safety policies and procedures are important (UK Safer Internet Centre, 2018[113]). A survey conducted in the United Kingdom showed that only 5% of schools did not have an online safety policy

in place. Yet for those schools that did, students were not always well-informed about this: only 74% of students were aware that they had an online safety policy at school; and few students were involved in writing online safety policies (Ofsted, 2014[112]). Listening to children and engaging them in the development of online safety policies is important, as children know best what new risks they are encountering on line.

Effective policies and procedures promote responsible and safe online practise for both students and staff (e.g. children knowing how to report an online safety incident; schools handling students' personal data in a safe and secure manner). Good policies are designed to support students' online learning rather than just preventing or limiting access. Policies and procedures should be up-to-date and integrated with other existing policies around anti-bullying, behaviour and safeguarding (UK Safer Internet Centre, 2018[113]).

Policies and rules to prevent cyberbullying should not be seen separately but within the context of traditional bullying. Many studies have shown strong correlations between traditional bullying and cyberbullying (Livingstone, Stoilova and Kelly, 2016[114]; Baldry, Farrington and Sorrentino, 2015[115]). Successful interventions to tackle traditional bullying may therefore also reduce cyberbullying (Livingstone, Stoilova and Kelly, 2016[114]). Effective policies for bullying clearly describe what behaviour is and is not accepted on line and at school, and what the consequences are for violating these rules (StopBullying, 2017[116]).

E-safety in the curriculum

Including online safety in the school's curriculum helps children become safe and responsible users of technologies (Hinduja and Patchin, 2018[117]). A survey conducted in the United Kingdom showed that 25% of secondary students could not recall "if they had been taught about online safety over the [previous] 12 months" (UK Safer Internet Centre, 2015[118]). Most schools use assemblies and ICT lessons to provide online safety education that focuses on teaching children digital skills and providing them with one-way online safety messages, as opposed to interactive and dynamic pedagogy (Harrison-Evans and Krasodomski-Jones, 2017[119]).

Due to a lack of evaluative evidence, it is unclear how effective such strategies are in supporting positive and safe online behaviour. In addition, there is a growing belief that schools should focus more on teaching children digital citizenship responsibilities. Children who are morally and ethically sensitive are more likely to engage in positive online behaviour, while the contrary is true for children with lower levels of moral sensitivity (Harrison-Evans and Krasodomski-Jones, 2017[119]). Peer-support programmes or mentoring schemes can also be effective in enhancing online safety in schools. Some 78% of 11-16 year-olds believe "young people have the power to create a kinder online community" (UK Safer Internet Centre, 2015[118]).

For adolescents and pre-teens, messages about online safety should include warnings about the risks of sexting and other online sexual risks. For example, education on sexting may be included within the school's sex and relationship education programme. Emphasising social risks (e.g. peer aggression or damaged reputation if an image goes viral) may contribute to "slut-shaming" and victim blaming, while focusing on education and career risks (e.g. rejection from educational or career opportunities if an image goes viral) may create unnecessary fear, as images are rarely uploaded to public websites (Hasinoff, 2012[120]). Instead, educators should focus on harm-reduction strategies that teach children empathy and digital privacy. This could include, for example, a classroom discussion about the benefits and risks of sharing sexy "selfies". If children know how to navigate sexual risk and trust, they will be less likely to get involved in acts of sexual violation (e.g. forwarding a sexual image of someone without permission) (Hasinoff, 2016[121]).

School communication with families

It is important that online safety education continues at home. As children go on line at an ever-younger age, parents and caregivers play a more important role in educating children about technology (Duerager and Livingstone, 2012[122]). Effective mediation reduces the likelihood of children being harmed by online risks or becoming "extreme Internet users" (Anderson, Steen and Stavropoulos, 2016[123]; Livingstone and Smith, 2014[124]).

It is therefore essential for schools to educate parents and caregivers as well as children. Parents lacking communication or digital skills may respond to safety incidents (e.g. cyberbullying) by taking their child's phone away. While this might be an effective short-term strategy, it can also prevent possibly harmed children from seeking help from their parents in the future (Fenaughty and Harré, 2013[125]). Developing relationships with families builds a safe community between home and school.

Technology can also be used as a tool to improve parent-teacher communication (Choi, 2018[126]). Through online platforms, parents can be informed about their child's attendance, performance and behaviour at school. Examples include

text messages to parents to engage them in their child's learning by informing them about the number of missed classes, providing students with career guidance and relevant tips for college admissions, or "mindset messages" to help students develop positive attitudes towards themselves, their peers and the school. These are low-cost and effective interventions that yield positive results (Escueta et al., 2017[127]). For teachers and school leaders, using technology (text messages, platforms and social networks) to make sure both parents have access to scholastic information and news about their child is efficient, and especially useful in ensuring that the information is transmitted in cases of divorce, when parents may be reluctant to communicate with each other.

THE ROLE OF PEERS

Besides seeking help from parents and teachers, children turn to each other when they need support; but the effectiveness of peer mediation remains little researched (Livingstone et al., 2011[128]). Some 44% of European 9-16 year-olds reported having received Internet safety advice from peers (as compared to 63% receiving advice from parents and 58% from teachers); 35% reported having given such advice to friends. Practical peer mediation appears to be even more common: 64% received help when they had trouble doing or finding something on line (Livingstone et al., 2011[128]).

Box 4.3. **Internet safety helplines**

Children who seek anonymous support can contact national helplines. Within the Insafe network (consisting of 31 countries), helplines provide children (and to a lesser extent parents and educators) with information, advice and emotional support about online safety. Most helplines can be accessed through diverse means, including telephone, e-mail, Skype, chat rooms and on line (Dinh et al., 2016[129]).

During the last quarter of 2017, 10 809 people contacted a helpline, 69% of whom were teenagers. Reasons for contacting helplines included cyberbullying (16%), relationships/sexuality (11%), sexting (8%), abuse of privacy (7%) and excessive use (6%) (Better Internet for Kids, 2018[130]). Internet safety helplines do not replace mediation of Internet use by parents, teachers or peers. Helplines should rather be seen as a first point of contact for immediate support (Dinh et al., 2016[129]).

Source: (Hooft Graafland, 2018[3])

Peer mediation can positively affect children's digital literacy and the type of activities they engage in on line. Children learn about new opportunities on line mainly through their peers. However, participating in creative online activities seems to depend less on peer support and more on children's individual priorities (Dinh et al., 2016[129]).

DEVELOPING POLICIES

Developing policies that both safeguard and empower children in a digital world is challenging. This section outlines different regulation strategies, as well as effective policy characteristics and recommendations. Also discussed are the gaps in our evidence base about children's lives on line that make it difficult to design policies that address risks and make the most of opportunities to benefit all children (for the full discussion, see (Hooft Graafland, 2018[3]).

Regulation strategies

The OECD's Directorate for Science, Technology and Industry is revisiting and updating the OECD (2012), Recommendation of the Council on the Protection of Children Online, https://legalinstruments.oecd.org/en/instruments/OECD-LEGAL-0389. The Recommendation includes principles for all stakeholders involved in making the Internet a safer environment for children and educating them to become responsible digital citizens.

For many risks that exist both on line and off-line, existing laws and regulations apply and no additional laws are needed. For such risks, most countries enhance general laws so that what is illegal off-line also becomes illegal on line. For example, a majority of countries have now updated their national regulation regarding child-inappropriate content to include the Internet.

In other cases, countries do adopt new legislation. In 2007, a new law was issued in France to make "happy slapping" – filming and distributing acts of violence on line (mostly carried out by youth) – a crime. In the United States, a law was adopted in 2003 on misleading online domain names. Australia, France, Ireland, Japan, New Zealand, Norway and the

United Kingdom have issued legislation related to cyber-grooming. In Japan, for example, it is now illegal to arrange dates with minors through online dating websites.

An alternative to direct governmental regulation to protect children on line is self- and co-regulation or using technologies. Self- and co-regulation measures influence the behaviour of market actors, such as search-engine operators and social media companies, that voluntarily show social responsibility, through codes of conduct, best practices or industry guidelines. Social network services, for instance, may contribute to online child safety by improving default privacy settings, introducing accessible "report abuse" buttons, or setting age limits for creating user accounts. Technological measures include filters (to keep children away from certain risks), age- or identity-verification systems (to prevent children from using specific websites) and walled gardens (to create child-safety zones on the Internet). Other policy tools include awareness campaigns that highlight online risks and opportunities, and provide positive content for children. Internet literacy is also increasingly becoming integrated in national educational systems (OECD, 2011[131]).

Common characteristics of successful policies

Besides protecting children from online harm, policy makers should support children in their digital skill development. (UNESCO, 2018[132]) compared five international studies on digital skills and identified two types of policies required to obtain an environment where children can successfully develop those skills. First, policy makers should focus on non-sectoral policies that support a digital environment and second, on sectoral policies related to education. Successful non-sectoral policies include those that improve technological infrastructure, digitalisation of businesses and the nature of online content.

Technological infrastructure refers to physical infrastructure and telecommunications networks (e.g. the costs, quality and speed of Internet access) and is essential for developing digital skills. Corporate digitalisation also contributes to skills development as education systems tend to adjust their teaching to meet labour-market requirements. If businesses demand more digital skills, students are more likely to develop these in school. In addition, the richness of online content can be a driver of digital skills development. In larger language communities (e.g. France, Germany, Spain, the United Kingdom and the United States) there is more positive online content for children available in their local language in comparison with smaller language communities (e.g. the Czech Republic, Greece and Slovenia) (Livingstone and Haddon, 2009[133]). Those children are likely to have more online opportunities and better digital skills (UNESCO, 2018[132]).

Education policies that foster the development of children's digital skills are those that provide ICT in schools, training for teachers, and support the integration of technologies into school curricula. The Republic of Korea and Singapore are good examples of how education policies can lead to higher levels of digital skills among schoolchildren. The growth strategy of the Republic of Korea includes massive investments in the so-called Smart Education Initiative since 2009 to digitalise education. Since 1997, Singapore has an ICT Master Plan for Education that reflects education policies related to improving children's digital skills. Other countries have adapted policies that go beyond teaching children basic technical skills. For example, in the United Kingdom, coding is now part of children's compulsory education. Students in Denmark can use the Internet while taking certain school examinations. The aim there is to teach children how to process and critically evaluate content rather than learning it by heart. In Norway, all students have to take a national digital skills evaluation test (UNESCO, 2018[132]).

Considerations for policy development

Even though children often seem to understand technology better than adults do, they need guidance on how to use technology in a responsible and positive way. The following set of messages are important to consider when developing policy (Hooft Graafland, 2018[3]):

- Adults who understand online safety and are able to use technology seem to be more successful in guiding children's digital use. Therefore, it is crucial that parents and teachers receive information on online safety and advice on how to help children manage online risks (Livingstone, Davidson and Bryce, 2017[134]).

- Children need to be stimulated to become content creators and not just receivers (Livingstone, Davidson and Bryce, 2017[134]). The Internet offers many opportunities for creativity and civic engagement, yet only 20% of children take advantage of them (Byrne and et al, 2016[135]). Most children still use the Internet for ready-made, mass-produced content, such as watching online video clips or listening to music.

- Empirical research has shown that children's socio-economic background and their level of digital skills are related such that children from more advantaged backgrounds tend to have higher digital skills. Special efforts should be made to overcome these inequalities and ensure that disadvantaged children receive the support and guidance they need to succeed in a digital world (Hatlevik, Guðmundsdóttir and Loi, 2015[136]; Hooft Graafland, 2018[3]).

- Children are the most frequent users of digital media and know best what new risks they are experiencing online. Policy makers and education practitioners should therefore actively listen to children and engage them in an ongoing conversion about how to use technologies in a responsible way (Third and et al, 2014[137]).

- Policy solutions to common challenges should be based on robust evidence. Although seemingly self-evident, this is not always the case, especially regarding current fears that technology is harmful for children. Policy makers should encourage quantitative and qualitative research, as this is vital to support claims regarding the impact of new technologies on children's behaviour and development (Byrne and Burton, 2017[138]).

CONCLUSIONS

While people have different views on the role that digital technology can and should play in schools, one cannot ignore how digital tools have fundamentally transformed the world outside of school. People who cannot navigate through the digital landscape can no longer participate fully in social, economic and cultural life. Technology should therefore play an important role in providing students with the 21st-century skills they need to succeed, and in providing teachers with learning environments that support 21st-century methods of teaching.

Claims that digital technologies will make teachers redundant seem generally unfounded. The heart of teaching has always been relational, and teaching seems to be one of the most enduring social activities. So there will be more, not less, demand for people who are able to build and support learners. The value of teaching as a key differentiator is only bound to rise as digitalisation leads to the unbundling of educational content, accreditation and teaching that make up traditional schools. In the digital age, the educational content of today will be a commodity available to everyone tomorrow. Accreditation still gives educational institutions enormous power; but what will micro-credentialing do to accreditation when employers can directly validate specific knowledge and skills? In the end, the quality of teaching seems the most valuable asset of modern educational institutions.

Still, as in many other professions, digital technologies will likely be used to perform many of the tasks now carried out by teachers. Even if teaching will never be digitised or outsourced, routine administrative and instructional tasks that take valuable time away from teaching are already being handed over to technology. Technology can elevate the role of teachers from imparting received knowledge towards working as co-creators of knowledge, as coaches, mentors and evaluators. Even today, intelligent digital learning systems can be adapted to suit personal learning styles.

Information and communication technology (ICT) is therefore changing the way children are learning. Not only schools, but also early childhood educational institutions are exploring ways to integrate ICT into the learning environment. But the availability of ICT in educational institutions is only one aspect of this shift. Education systems need to re-evaluate their curricula, and teachers need to reassess their teaching styles, to ensure that ICT is used effectively. Education policies that foster the development of children's digital skills are those that provide ICT in schools, training for teachers, and support the integration of technologies into school curricula.

At the same time, given the ubiquity of technology in the lives of 21st-century children, a concerted effort needs to be made to protect children from the risks associated with technology use, including cyberbullying, phishing, access to unsuitable material and pornography, and "grooming" by strangers. But parents and educators should keep in mind the potential benefits of ICT use, such as forming and sustaining friendships, developing digital skills relevant for the 21st-century labour market and accessing nearly limitless information.

Notes

1. This was previously thought to be 700-1 000, and was updated by the Center on the Developing Child at Harvard University in 2017.

2. Magnetic resonance imaging refers to producing structural images of organs, such as the brain/central nervous system; functional magnetic resonance imaging detects changes in blood flow following enhanced neural activity from task-induced cognitive changes or as a result of "unregulated processes in the resting brain" (Logothetis, 2008[31]; Glover, 2011[30]).

References

Afifi, T. et al. (2018), "WIRED: The impact of media and technology use on stress (cortisol) and inflammation (interleukin IL-6) in fast paced families", *Computers in Human Behavior*, Vol. 81, pp. 265-273, http://dx.doi.org/10.1016/j.chb.2017.12.010.   [87]

Anderson, D. et al (2001), "Early childhood television viewing and adolescent behavior: the recontact study", *Monographs of the Society for Research in Child Development*, Vol. 66/1, pp. 1-47, http://www.ncbi.nlm.nih.gov/pubmed/11326591.   [47]

Anderson, D. (1998), "Educational Television is not an Oxymoron", *The ANNALS of the American Academy of Political and Social Science*, Vol. 557/1, pp. 24-38, http://dx.doi.org/10.1177/0002716298557000003.   [46]

Anderson, D. and T. Pempek (2005), "Television and Very Young Children", *American Behavioral Scientist*, Vol. 48/5, pp. 505-522, http://dx.doi.org/10.1177/0002764204271506.   [54]

Anderson, D. and K. Subrahmanyam (2017), "Digital Screen Media and Cognitive Development on behalf of the Cognitive Impacts of Digital Media Workgroup", *Pediatrics*, Vol. 140/2, http://pediatrics.aappublications.org/content/pediatrics/140/Supplement_2/S57.full.pdf.   [45]

Anderson, E., E. Steen and V. Stavropoulos (2016), "Internet use and Problematic Internet Use: a systematic review of longitudinal research trends in adolescence and emergent adulthood", *International Journal of Adolescence and Youth*, Vol. 22/4, pp. 430-454, http://dx.doi.org/10.1080/02673843.2016.1227716.   [120]

Arora, T. et al. (2014), "Associations between specific technologies and adolescent sleep quantity, sleep quality, and parasomnias", *Sleep Medicine*, Vol. 15/2, pp. 240-247, http://dx.doi.org/10.1016/j.sleep.2013.08.799.   [83]

Axford, C., A. Joosten and C. Harris (2018), "iPad applications that required a range of motor skills promoted motor coordination in children commencing primary school", *Australian Occupational Therapy Journal*, Vol. 65/2, pp. 146-155, http://dx.doi.org/10.1111/1440-1630.12450.   [100]

Baldry, A., D. Farrington and A. Sorrentino (2015), ""Am I at risk of cyberbullying"? A narrative review and conceptual framework for research on risk of cyberbullying and cybervictimization: The risk and needs assessment approach", *Aggression and Violent Behavior*, Vol. 23, pp. 36-51, http://dx.doi.org/10.1016/j.avb.2015.05.014.   [112]

Baranowski, T. et al. (2012), "Impact of an Active Video Game on Healthy Children's Physical Activity", *PEDIATRICS*, Vol. 129/3, pp. e636-e642, http://dx.doi.org/10.1542/peds.2011-2050.   [101]

Barkovich, T. (1988), "Normal maturation of the neonatal and infant brain: MR imaging at 1.5 T.", *Radiology*, Vol. 166/1, pp. 173-180, http://dx.doi.org/10.1148/radiology.166.1.3336675.   [20]

Barr, R. et al. (2008), "Infants' Attention and Responsiveness to Television Increases With Prior Exposure and Parental Interaction", *Infancy*, Vol. 13/1, pp. 30-56, http://dx.doi.org/10.1080/15250000701779378.   [40]

Bavelier, D., C. Green and M. Dye (2010), "Children, wired: For better and for worse", *Neuron*, Vol. 67/5, pp. 692-701, http://dx.doi.org/10.1016/J.NEURON.2010.08.035.   [16]

Bellissimo, N. et al. (2007), "Effect of Television Viewing at Mealtime on Food Intake After a Glucose Preload in Boys", *Pediatric Research*, Vol. 61/6, pp. 745-749, http://dx.doi.org/10.1203/pdr.0b013e3180536591.   [92]

Bergmann, J. and A. Sams (2012), *Flip Your Classroom: Reach Every Student in Every Class Every Day, International Society for Technology in Education*, https://www.liceopalmieri.edu.it/wp-content/uploads/2016/11/Flip-Your-Classroom.pdf (accessed on 9 August 2018).   [7]

Better Internet for Kids (2018), *Latest helpline trends: Quarter 4*, http://www.betterinternetforkids.eu/web/portal/practice/helplines/detail?articleId=2942283 (accessed on 25 June 2018).   [127]

Bliss, T. and R. Schoepfer (2004), "Neuroscience: controlling the ups and downs of synaptic strength", *Scienc*, Vol. 304/5673, pp. 973-974, http://dx.doi.org/10.1126/science.1098805.   [21]

Bonetti, L., M. Campbell and L. Gilmore (2010), "The Relationship of Loneliness and Social Anxiety with Children's and Adolescents' Online Communication", *Cyberpsychology, Behavior, and Social Networking*, Vol. 13/3, pp. 279-285, http://dx.doi.org/10.1089/cyber.2009.0215. [73]

Boniel-Nissim, M. et al. (2014), "Supportive communication with parents moderates the negative effects of electronic media use on life satisfaction during adolescence", *International Journal of Public Health*, Vol. 60/2, pp. 189-198, http://dx.doi.org/10.1007/s00038-014-0636-9. [77]

Brainard, G. and J. Hanifin (2002), "Action Spectrum for Melatonin Suppression: Evidence for a Novel Circadian Photoreceptor in the Human Eye", in *Biologic Effects of Light 2001*, Springer US, Boston, MA, http://dx.doi.org/10.1007/978-1-4615-0937-0_45. [79]

Brody, J. (2015), "Screen Addiction Is Taking a Toll on Children", *New York Times*, https://well.blogs.nytimes.com/2015/07/06/screen-addiction-is-taking-a-toll-on-children/?_r=0. [4]

Bulman, G. and R. Farlie (2016), "Technology and education: Computers, software, and the Internet", in *Handbook of Economics of Education, Vol. 5*, http://dx.doi.org/10.1016/B978-0-444-63459-7.00005-1. [10]

Byrne, J. and P. Burton (2017), "Children as Internet users: how can evidence better inform policy debate?", *Journal of Cyber Policy*, Vol. 2/1, pp. 39-52, http://dx.doi.org/10.1080/23738871.2017.1291698. [135]

Byrne, J. and et al (2016), *Global Kids Online Research synthesis, 2015-2016*, UNICEF Office of Research– Innocenti and London School of Economics and Political Science, http://eprints.lse.ac.uk/67965/7/Global%20Kids%20Online_Synthesis%20report_2016.pdf. [132]

Canadian Paediatric Society, Digital Health Task Force, Ottawa, Ontario (2017), "Screen time and young children: Promoting health and development in a digital world", *Paediatrics & Child Health*, Vol. 22/8, pp. 461-468, http://dx.doi.org/10.1093/pch/pxx123. [42]

Center on the Developing Child (2009), *Five Numbers to Remember About Early Childhood Development*, http://www.developingchild.harvard.edu. [23]

Certain, L. and R. Kahn (2002), "Prevalence, correlates, and trajectory of television viewing among infants and toddlers", *Pediatrics*, Vol. 109/4, pp. 634-42, http://www.ncbi.nlm.nih.gov/pubmed/11927700. [43]

Choi, A. (2018), "Emotional well-being of children and adolescents: Recent trends and relevant factors", *OECD Education Working Papers*, No. 169, OECD Publishing, Paris, https://dx.doi.org/10.1787/41576fb2-en. [123]

Ciccarelli, M. (2015), "Managing children's postural risk when using mobile technology at home: Challenges and strategies", *Applied Ergonomics*, Vol. 51, pp. 189-198, http://dx.doi.org/10.1016/J.APERGO.2015.04.003. [103]

Crone, E. and E. Konjin (2018), "Media use and brain development during adolescence", *Nature Communications*, Vol. 9/1, p. 588, http://dx.doi.org/10.1038/s41467-018-03126-x. [24]

Davidson, R. and W. Irwin (1999), "The functional neuroanatomy of emotion and affective style", *Trends in Cognitive Sciences*, Vol. 3/1, pp. 11-21, http://dx.doi.org/10.1016/s1364-6613(98)01265-0. [88]

Dinh, T. et al. (2016), *Insafe Helplines: Operations, effectiveness and emerging issues for internet safety helplines*, Insafe, European Schoolnet, http://www.betterinternetforkids.eu/documents/167024/507884/Helpline+Fund+Report+-+Final/4cf8f03a-3a48-4365-af76-f03e01cb505d. [126]

Duerager, A. and S. Livingstone (2012), *How can parents support children's internet safety?*, http://www.lse.ac.uk/media%40lse/research/EUKidsOnline/EU%20Kids%20III/Reports/ParentalMediation.pdf (accessed on 30 March 2018). [119]

Duggan, M. and A. Smith (2014), *Social Media Update*, Pew Research Center, http://www.pewinternet.org/2013/12/30/social-media-update-2013/. [66]

Durkee, T. (2012), "Prevalence of pathological internet use among adolescents in Europe: demographic and social factors", *Addiction*, Vol. 107/12, pp. 2210-2222, http://dx.doi.org/10.1111/j.1360-0443.2012.03946.x. [14]

Escueta, M. et al. (2017), *Education Technology: An Evidence-Based Review*, National Bureau of Economic Research , Cambridge, MA, http://dx.doi.org/10.3386/w23744. [124]

Evans Schmidt, M. and D. Anderson (2009), "The impact of television on cognitive development and educational achievement", in *Children and Television: Fifty years of research*, Erlbaum, Mahwah, NJ. [37]

Fairlie, R. and A. Kalil (2017), "The effects of computers on children's social development and school participation: Evidence from a randomized control experiment", *Economics of Education Review*, Vol. 57, pp. 10-19, http://dx.doi.org/10.1016/j.econedurev.2017.01.001. [76]

Falck, O., C. Mang and L. Woessman (2018), "Virtually no effect? Different uses of classroom computers and their effects on student achievement", *Oxford Bulletin of Economics and Statistics*, Vol. 80/1, pp. 1-38, http://dx.doi.org/10.1111/obes.12192. [11]

Fenaughty, J. and N. Harré (2013), "Factors associated with distressing electronic harassment and cyberbullying", *Computers in Human Behavior*, Vol. 29/3, pp. 803-811, http://dx.doi.org/10.1016/j.chb.2012.11.008. [122]

Figueiro, M. and D. Overington (2016), "Self-luminous devices and melatonin suppression in adolescents", *Lighting Research & Technology*, Vol. 48/8, pp. 966-975, http://dx.doi.org/10.1177/1477153515584979. [81]

Foster, E. and S. Watkins (2010), "The Value of Reanalysis: TV Viewing and Attention Problems", *Child Development*, Vol. 81/1, pp. 368-375, http://dx.doi.org/10.1111/j.1467-8624.2009.01400.x. [34]

Franceschini, S. et al. (2017), "Action video games improve reading abilities and visual-to-auditory attentional shifting in English-speaking children with dyslexia", *Scientific Reports*, Vol. 7/1, http://dx.doi.org/10.1038/s41598-017-05826-8. [59]

Fuhrmann, D., L. Knoll and S. Blakemore (2015), "Adolescence as a Sensitive Period of Brain Development", *Trends in Cognitive Sciences*, Vol. 19/10, pp. 558-566, http://dx.doi.org/10.1016/J.TICS.2015.07.008. [29]

Gao, Z. et al. (2015), "A meta-analysis of active video games on health outcomes among children and adolescents", *Obesity Reviews*, Vol. 16/9, pp. 783-794, http://dx.doi.org/10.1111/obr.12287. [99]

Gebremariam, M. et al. (2013), "Are screen-based sedentary behaviors longitudinally associated with dietary behaviors and leisure-time physical activity in the transition into adolescence?", *International Journal of Behavioral Nutrition and Physical Activity*, Vol. 10/1, p. 9, http://dx.doi.org/10.1186/1479-5868-10-9. [94]

Glover, G. (2011), "Overview of functional magnetic resonance imaging", *Neurosurgery clinics of North America*, Vol. 22/2, pp. 133-139, http://dx.doi.org/10.1016/j.nec.2010.11.001. [30]

Gottschalk, F. (2019), "Impacts of technology use on children: Exploring literature on the brain, cognition and well-being", *OECD Education Working Papers*, No. 195, OECD Publishing, Paris, https://dx.doi.org/10.1787/8296464e-en. [6]

Granic, I., A. Lobel and R. Engels (2014), "The benefits of playing video games.", *American Psychologist*, Vol. 69/1, pp. 66-78, http://dx.doi.org/10.1037/a0034857. [56]

Hale, L. and S. Guan (2015), "Screen time and sleep among school-aged children and adolescents: A systematic literature review", *Sleep Medicine Reviews*, Vol. 21, pp. 50-58, http://dx.doi.org/10.1016/j.smrv.2014.07.007. [82]

Harris, C. (2015), "Children, computer exposure and musculoskeletal outcomes: the development of pathway models for school and home computer-related musculoskeletal outcomes", *Ergonomics*, Vol. 58/10, pp. 1611-1623, http://dx.doi.org/10.1080/00140139.2015.1035762. [105]

Harrison-Evans, P. and A. Krasodomski-Jones (2017), *The Moral Web: Youth Character, Ethics and Behaviour*, https://www.demos.co.uk/project/the-moral-web/ (accessed on 15 May 2018). [116]

Hasinoff, A. (2016), *Tips for parents and educators*, https://amyhasinoff.wordpress.com/tips-for-parents-educators/ (accessed on 17 May 2018). [118]

Hasinoff, A. (2012), "Sexting as media production: Rethinking social media and sexuality", *New Media & Society*, Vol. 15/4, pp. 449-465, http://dx.doi.org/10.1177/1461444812459171. [117]

Hatlevik, O., G. Guðmundsdóttir and M. Loi (2015), "Digital diversity among upper secondary students: A multilevel analysis of the relationship between cultural capital, self-efficacy, strategic use of information and digital competence", *Computers & Education*, Vol. 81, pp. 345-353, http://dx.doi.org/10.1016/j.compedu.2014.10.019. [133]

Hattie, J. and G. Yates (2013), *Visible Learning and the Science of How We Learn*, Routledge, London. [8]

Haughton, C., M. Aiken and C. Cheevers (2015), "Cyber Babies: The Impact of Emerging Technology on the Developing Infant", *Psychology Research*, Vol. 5/9, pp. 504-518, http://dx.doi.org/10.17265/2159-5542/2015.09.002. [36]

Hinduja, S. and J. Patchin (2018), *Cyberbullying fact sheet: Identification, Prevention, and Response*, https://cyberbullying.org/Cyberbullying-Identification-Prevention-Response-2018.pdf (accessed on 16 May 2018). [114]

Hooft Graafland, J. (2018), "New technologies and 21st century children: Recent trends and outcomes", *OECD Education Working Papers*, No. 179, OECD Publishing, Paris, https://dx.doi.org/10.1787/e071a505-en. [3]

Hopkins, L., F. Brookes and J. Green (2013), "Books, bytes and brains: The implications of new knowledge for children's early literacy learning", *Australasian Journal of Early Childhood*, Vol. 38/1, pp. 23-28, https://search.informit.com.au/documentSummary;dn=266659007690976;res=IELHSS. [5]

Irwin, L., A. Siddiqi and C. Hertzman (2007), *Early Child Development : A Powerful Equalizer Final Report*, World Health Organization's Commission on the Social Determinants of Health. [27]

Jacobs, K. and N. Baker (2002), "The association between children's computer use and musculoskeletal discomfort", *Work*, Vol. 18/3, pp. 221-226. [102]

Juster, R., B. McEwen and S. Lupien (2010), "Allostatic load biomarkers of chronic stress and impact on health and cognition", *Neuroscience & Biobehavioral Reviews*, Vol. 35/1, pp. 2-16, http://dx.doi.org/10.1016/j.neubiorev.2009.10.002. [86]

Kardfelt-Winther, D. (2017), "How does the time children spend using digital technology impact their mental well-being, social relationships and physical activity? An evidence-focused literature review"", *Innocenti Discussion Paper 2017-02*, UNICEF Office of Research – Innocenti, Florence, https://www.unicef-irc.org/publications/pdf/Children-digital-technology-wellbeing.pdf. [63]

Kaveri Subrahmanyam and Patricia Greenfield (2008), "Online Communication and Adolescent Relationships", *The Future of Children*, Vol. 18/1, pp. 119-146, http://dx.doi.org/10.1353/foc.0.0006. [107]

Kostyrka-Allchorne, K., N. Cooper and A. Simpson (2017), "The relationship between television exposure and children's cognition and behaviour: A systematic review", *Developmental Review*, Vol. 44, pp. 19-58, http://dx.doi.org/10.1016/j.dr.2016.12.002. [53]

Kraut, R. et al (1998), "Internet paradox. A social technology that reduces social involvement and psychological well-being?", *The American Psychologist*, Vol. 53/9, pp. 1017-1031, http://www.ncbi.nlm.nih.gov/pubmed/9841579. [71]

Kuhl, P., F. Tsao and H. Liu (2003), "Foreign-language experience in infancy: Effects of short-term exposure and social interaction on phonetic learning", *Proceedings of the National Academy of Sciences*, Vol. 100/15, pp. 9096-9101, http://dx.doi.org/10.1073/pnas.1532872100. [55]

Landhuis, C. (2007), "Does Childhood Television Viewing Lead to Attention Problems in Adolescence? Results From a Prospective Longitudinal Study", *Pediatrics*, Vol. 120/3, pp. 532-537, http://dx.doi.org/10.1542/peds.2007-0978. [32]

Lane, R. and L. Nadel (eds.) (2000), *A Second Chance for Emotions*, Oxford University Press, New York. [89]

Lee, E., J. Spence and V. Carson (2017), "Television viewing, reading, physical activity and brain development among young South Korean children", *Journal of Science and Medicine in Sport*, Vol. 20/7, pp. 672-677, http://dx.doi.org/10.1016/j.jsams.2016.11.014. [41]

Lenhart, A. (2015), *Teens, Technology and Friendships*, Pew Research Center, http://www.pewinternet.org/2015/08/06/teens-technology-and-friendships/. [67]

Leung, L. (2007), "Stressful Life Events, Motives for Internet Use, and Social Support Among Digital Kids", *CyberPsychology & Behavior*, Vol. 10/2, pp. 204-214, http://dx.doi.org/10.1089/cpb.2006.9967. [91]

Linebarger, D. and J. Piotrowski (2009), "TV as storyteller: How exposure to television narratives impacts at-risk preschoolers' story knowledge and narrative skills", *British Journal of Developmental Psychology*, Vol. 27/1, pp. 47-69, http://dx.doi.org/10.1348/026151008x400445. [51]

Linebarger, D. and S. Vaala (2010), "Screen media and language development in infants and toddlers: An ecological perspective", *Developmental Review*, Vol. 30/2, pp. 176-202, http://dx.doi.org/10.1016/j.dr.2010.03.006. [49]

Linebarger, D. and D. Walker (2005), "Infants' and Toddlers' Television Viewing and Language Outcomes", *American Behavioral Scientist*, Vol. 48/5, pp. 624-645, http://dx.doi.org/10.1177/0002764204271505. [50]

Livingstone, S., J. Davidson and J. Bryce (2017), *Children's online activities, risks and safety: A literature review by the UKCCIS Evidence Group*, UK Council for Children Internet Safety, London, https://assets.publishing.service.gov.uk/government/uploads/system/uploads/attachment_data/file/650933/Literature_Review_Final_October_2017.pdf. [131]

Livingstone, S. and L. Haddon (2009), "EU Kids Online: Final report", *EU Kids Online (EC Safer Internet Plus Programme Deliverable D6.5)*, LSE, London, http://uploadi.www.ris.org/editor/1273341021EUKidsOnlineFinalReport.pdf. [130]

Livingstone, S. et al. (2011), *Risks and safety on the internet: the perspective of European children: full findings and policy implications from the EU Kids Online survey of 9-16 year olds and their parents in 25 countries,*, EU Kids Online, Deliverable D4. EU Kids Online Network, http://eprints.lse.ac.uk/33731/. [125]

Livingstone, S. and P. Smith (2014), "Annual Research Review: Harms experienced by child users of online and mobile technologies: the nature, prevalence and management of sexual and aggressive risks in the digital age", *Journal of Child Psychology and Psychiatry*, Vol. 55/6, pp. 635-654, http://dx.doi.org/10.1111/jcpp.12197. [121]

Livingstone, S., M. Stoilova and A. Kelly (2016), "Cyberbullying: incidence, trends and consequence", in *Ending the Torment: Tackling Bullying from the Schoolyard to Cyberspace*, United Nations Office of the Special Representative of the Secretary-General on Violence against Children, New York, http://eprints.lse.ac.uk/68079/. [111]

Logothetis, N. (2008), "What we can do and what we cannot do with fMRI", *Nature*, Vol. 453/7197, pp. 869-878, http://dx.doi.org/10.1038/nature06976. [31]

Luciana, M. (2013), "Adolescent brain development in normality and psychopathology", *Development and Psychopathology*, Vol. 25/4pt2, pp. 1325-1345, http://dx.doi.org/10.1017/S0954579413000643. [25]

Meshi, D., D. Tamir and H. Heekeren (2015), "The Emerging Neuroscience of Social Media", *Trends in Cognitive Sciences*, Vol. 19/12, pp. 771-782, http://dx.doi.org/10.1016/j.tics.2015.09.004. [65]

Middaugh, E., L. Clark and P. Ballard (2017), "Digital Media, Participatory Politics, and Positive Youth Development", *Pediatrics*, Vol. 140/Supplement 2, pp. S127-S131, http://dx.doi.org/10.1542/peds.2016-1758q. [108]

Miller, B. and R. Morris (2016), "Virtual Peer Effects in Social Learning Theory", *Crime & Delinquency*, Vol. 62/12, pp. 1543-1569, http://dx.doi.org/10.1177/0011128714526499. [75]

Ministère des Solidarités et de la Santé (2018), *Carnet de Santé (health booklet)*, http://solidarites-sante.gouv.fr/IMG/pdf/carnet_de_sante-num-.pdf. [17]

Murphy, S., P. Buckle and D. Stubbs (2004), "Classroom posture and self-reported back and neck pain in schoolchildren", *Applied Ergonomics*, Vol. 35/2, pp. 113-120, http://dx.doi.org/10.1016/J.APERGO.2004.01.001. [106]

Neuman, S. (1988), "The Displacement Effect: Assessing the Relation between Television Viewing and Reading Performance", *Reading Research Quarterly*, Vol. 23/4, p. 414, http://dx.doi.org/10.2307/747641. [93]

Norris, E., M. Hamer and E. Stamatakis (2016), "Active Video Games in Schools and Effects on Physical Activity and Health: A Systematic Review", *The Journal of Pediatrics*, Vol. 172, pp. 40-46.e5, http://dx.doi.org/10.1016/j.jpeds.2016.02.001. [98]

OECD (2019), *Trends Shaping Education 2019*, OECD Publishing, Paris, https://dx.doi.org/10.1787/trends_edu-2019-en. [13]

OECD (2018), *Children and Young People's Mental Health in the Digital Age: Shaping the Future*, http://www.oecd.org/els/health-systems/Children-and-Young-People-Mental-Health-in-the-Digital-Age.pdf. [64]

OECD (2017), *PISA 2015 Results (Volume III): Students' Well-Being*, PISA, OECD Publishing, Paris, https://dx.doi.org/10.1787/9789264273856-en. [1]

OECD (2015), *Students, Computers and Learning: Making the Connection*, PISA, OECD Publishing, Paris, https://dx.doi.org/10.1787/9789264239555-en. [2]

OECD (2011), "The Protection of Children Online: Risks Faced by Children Online and Policies to Protect Them", *OECD Digital Economy Papers*, No. 179, OECD Publishing, Paris, https://dx.doi.org/10.1787/5kgcjf71pl28-en. [128]

Ofcom (2019), *Children and Parents: Media Use and Attitudes Report 2018*, https://www.ofcom.org.uk/research-and-data/media-literacy-research/childrens/children-and-parents-media-use-and-attitudes-report-2018. [15]

Ofsted (2014), *Inspecting e-safety in schools*, The Office for Standards in Education, Children's Services and Skills (Ofsted), http://dwn5wtkv5mp2x.cloudfront.net/downloads/resources/Ofsted_-_Inspecting_e-safety.pdf. [109]

Orben, A. and A. Przylbylski (2019), "The association between adolescent well-being and digital technology use", *Nature Human Behavior*, Vol. 3/2, http://dx.doi.org/10.1038/s41562-018-0506-1. [19]

Paniagua, A. and D. Istance (2018), *Teachers as Designers of Learning Environments: The Importance of Innovative Pedagogies*, Educational Research and Innovation, OECD Publishing, Paris, https://dx.doi.org/10.1787/9789264085374-en. [9]

Parkes, A. (2013), "Do television and electronic games predict children's psychosocial adjustment? Longitudinal research using the UK Millennium Cohort Study", *Archives of Disease in Childhood*, Vol. 98/5880, pp. 341-8, http://dx.doi.org/10.1136/archdischild-2011-301508. [35]

Pasek, J. et al. (2006), "America's Youth and Community Engagement", *Communication Research*, Vol. 33/3, pp. 115-135, http://dx.doi.org/10.1177/0093650206287073. [97]

Pastalkova, E. (2006), "Storage of Spatial Information by the Maintenance Mechanism of LTP", *Science*, Vol. 313/5790, pp. 1141-1144, http://dx.doi.org/10.1126/science.1128657. [22]

Paus, T. (2005), "Mapping brain maturation and cognitive development during adolescence", *Trends in Cognitive Sciences*, Vol. 9/2, pp. 60-68, http://dx.doi.org/10.1016/J.TICS.2004.12.008. [26]

Petanjek, Z. (2011), "Extraordinary neoteny of synaptic spines in the human prefrontal cortex", *Proceedings of the National Academy of Sciences of the United States of America*, Vol. 108/32, pp. 13281-6, http://dx.doi.org/10.1073/pnas.1105108108. [28]

Pew Research Center (2018), *Teens, Social Media and Technology 2018*, http://www.pewinternet.org/2018/05/31/teens-social-media-technology-2018/. [68]

Pujol, J. et al. (2016), "Video gaming in school children: How much is enough?", *Annals of Neurology*, Vol. 80/3, pp. 424-433, http://dx.doi.org/10.1002/ana.24745. [58]

Rideout, V. and E. Hamel (2006), *The Media Family: Electronic Media in the Lives of infants, Toddlers, Preschoolers and their Parents*, Kaiser Family Foundation, https://kaiserfamilyfoundation.files.wordpress.com/2013/01/zero-to-six-electronic-media-in-the-lives-of-infants-toddlers-and-preschoolers-pdf.pdf. [44]

Rodrigues, M. and F. Biagi (2017), *Digital Technologies and Learning Outcomes of Students from Low Socio-economic Background: An Analysis of PISA 2015*, Publications Office of the European Union, Luxembourg, http://dx.doi.org/10.2760/415251. [12]

Romer, D., Z. Bagdasarov and E. More (2013), "Older Versus Newer Media and the Well-being of United States Youth: Results From a National Longitudinal Panel", *Journal of Adolescent Health*, Vol. 52/5, pp. 613-619, http://dx.doi.org/10.1016/j.jadohealth.2012.11.012. [95]

Romer, D., K. Jamieson and J. Pasek (2009), "Building Social Capital in Young People: The Role of Mass Media and Life Outlook", *Political Communication*, Vol. 26/1, pp. 65-83, http://dx.doi.org/10.1080/10584600802622878. [96]

Rueda, M. et al (2005), "Training, maturation, and genetic influences on the development of executive attention", *PNAS*, Vol. 102/41, pp. 14931-14936, https://www.ncbi.nlm.nih.gov/pmc/articles/PMC1253585/pdf/pnas-0506897102.pdf. [38]

Schmidt, M. and D. Anderson (2007), "The impact of television on cognitive development and educational achievement", In Murray, N. and E. Wartella (eds.), *Children and television: 50 years of Research*, Lawrence Erlbaum, Manwah, NJ. [48]

Sherman, L. et al. (2016), "The Power of the Like in Adolescence", *Psychological Science*, Vol. 27/7, pp. 1027-1035, http://dx.doi.org/10.1177/0956797616645673. [70]

Smahel, D. (2012), *Excessive internet use among European children Report Original citation: Excessive Internet Use among European Children*, London School of Economics & Political Science, http://eprints.lse.ac.uk/47344/1/Excessive%20internet%20use.pdf. [62]

Stepanski, E. and J. Wyatt (2003), "Use of sleep hygiene in the treatment of insomnia", *Sleep Medicine Reviews*, Vol. 7/3, pp. 215-225. [85]

StopBullying (2017), *Set Policies & Rules*, https://www.stopbullying.gov/prevention/at-school/rules/index.html (accessed on 23 May 2018). [113]

Straker, L. (2017), "Mobile technology dominates school children's IT use in an advantaged school community and is associated with musculoskeletal and visual symptoms", *Ergonomics*, pp. 1-12, http://dx.doi.org/10.1080/00140139.2017.1401671. [104]

Takeuchi, H. et al. (2013), "The Impact of Television Viewing on Brain Structures: Cross-Sectional and Longitudinal Analyses", *Cerebral Cortex*, Vol. 25/5, pp. 1188-1197, http://dx.doi.org/10.1093/cercor/bht315. [39]

Thapan, K., J. Arendt and D. Skene (2001), "An action spectrum for melatonin suppression: evidence for a novel non-rod, non-cone photoreceptor system in humans", *The Journal of Physiology*, Vol. 535/1, pp. 261-267, http://dx.doi.org/10.1111/j.1469-7793.2001.t01-1-00261.x. [80]

The IMAGEN Consortium (2011), Kuhn et al., "The neural basis of video gaming", *Translational Psychiatry*, Vol. 1/11, pp. e53-e53, http://dx.doi.org/10.1038/tp.2011.53. [57]

Third, A. and et al (2014), *Children's Rights in the Digital Age: A Download from Children Around the World*, Young and Well Cooperative Research Centre, Melbourne, http://www.unicef.org/publications/files/Childrens_Rights_in_the_Digital_Age_A_Download_from_Children_Around_the_World_FINAL.pdf. [134]

Touitou, Y., D. Touitou and A. Reinberg (2016), "Disruption of adolescents' circadian clock: The vicious circle of media use, exposure to light at night, sleep loss and risk behaviors", *Journal of Physiology-Paris*, Vol. 110/4, pp. 467-479, http://dx.doi.org/10.1016/j.jphysparis.2017.05.001. [78]

Turel, O. et al. (2014), "Examination of Neural Systems Sub-Serving Facebook "Addiction"", *Psychological Reports*, Vol. 115/3, pp. 675-695, http://dx.doi.org/10.2466/18.pr0.115c31z8. [60]

UK Safer Internet Centre (2018), *Online Safety Policy*, https://www.saferinternet.org.uk/advice-centre/teachers-and-school-staff/online-safety-policy (accessed on 23 May 2018). [110]

UK Safer Internet Centre (2015), *Ofsted reveals new 'Online Safety in Schools' survey | Safer Internet Centre*, https://www.saferinternet.org.uk/blog/ofsted-reveals-new-%E2%80%98online-safety-schools%E2%80%99-survey (accessed on 23 May 2018). [115]

UNESCO (2018), "Managing tomorrow's digital skills: what conclusions can we draw from international comparative indicators?", *UNESCO Working Papers on Education Policy*, UNESCO Publishing, Paris, http://unesdoc.unesco.org/images/0026/002618/261853e.pdf. [129]

UNICEF (2017), *The State of the World's Children: Children in a digital world*, https://www.unicef.org/publications/files/SOWC_2017_ENG_WEB.pdf (accessed on 22 February 2018). [72]

Valkenburg, P. and J. Peter (2007), "Online Communication and Adolescent Well-Being: Testing the Stimulation Versus the Displacement Hypothesis", *Journal of Computer-Mediated Communication*, Vol. 12/4, pp. 1169-1182, http://dx.doi.org/10.1111/j.1083-6101.2007.00368.x. [74]

van der Lely, S. et al. (2015), "Blue Blocker Glasses as a Countermeasure for Alerting Effects of Evening Light-Emitting Diode Screen Exposure in Male Teenagers", *Journal of Adolescent Health*, Vol. 56/1, pp. 113-119, http://dx.doi.org/10.1016/j.jadohealth.2014.08.002. [84]

Viner, R., M. Davie and A. Firth (2019), *The Health Impacts of Screen Time: A Guide for Clinicians and Parents*, RCPCH, London, https://www.rcpch.ac.uk/sites/default/files/2018-12/rcpch_screen_time_guide_-_final.pdf. [18]

Wallenius, M. et al. (2010), "Salivary Cortisol in Relation to the Use of Information and Communication Technology (ICT) in School-Aged Children", *Psychology*, Vol. 01/02, pp. 88-95, http://dx.doi.org/10.4236/psych.2010.12012. [90]

Weinstein, A. and M. Lejoyeux (2015), "New developments on the neurobiological and pharmaco-genetic mechanisms underlying internet and videogame addiction", *The American Journal on Addictions*, Vol. 24/2, pp. 117-125, http://dx.doi.org/10.1111/ajad.12110. [61]

Woods, H. and H. Scott (2016), "#Sleepyteens: Social media use in adolescence is associated with poor sleep quality, anxiety, depression and low self-esteem", *Journal of Adolescence*, Vol. 51, pp. 41-49, http://dx.doi.org/10.1016/j.adolescence.2016.05.008. [69]

Wright, J. et al. (2001), "The Relations of Early Television Viewing to School Readiness and Vocabulary of Children from Low-Income Families: The Early Window Project", *Child Development*, Vol. 72/5, pp. 1347-1366, http://dx.doi.org/10.1111/1467-8624.t01-1-00352. [52]

Zimmerman, F. and D. Christakis (2005), "Children's television viewing and cognitive outcomes", *Archives of Pediatrics & Adolescent Medicine*, Vol. 159/7, p. 619, http://dx.doi.org/10.1001/archpedi.159.7.619. [33]

ORGANISATION FOR ECONOMIC CO-OPERATION AND DEVELOPMENT

The OECD is a unique forum where governments work together to address the economic, social and environmental challenges of globalisation. The OECD is also at the forefront of efforts to understand and to help governments respond to new developments and concerns, such as corporate governance, the information economy and the challenges of an ageing population. The Organisation provides a setting where governments can compare policy experiences, seek answers to common problems, identify good practice and work to co-ordinate domestic and international policies.

The OECD member countries are: Australia, Austria, Belgium, Canada, Chile, the Czech Republic, Denmark, Estonia, Finland, France, Germany, Greece, Hungary, Iceland, Ireland, Israel, Italy, Japan, Korea, Latvia, Lithuania, Luxembourg, Mexico, the Netherlands, New Zealand, Norway, Poland, Portugal, the Slovak Republic, Slovenia, Spain, Sweden, Switzerland, Turkey, the United Kingdom and the United States. The European Union takes part in the work of the OECD.

OECD Publishing disseminates widely the results of the Organisation's statistics gathering and research on economic, social and environmental issues, as well as the conventions, guidelines and standards agreed by its members.

OECD PUBLISHING, 2, rue André-Pascal, 75775 PARIS CEDEX 16
(91 2019 04 1 P) ISBN 978-92-64-31386-6 – 2019

Printed by Libri Plureos GmbH in Hamburg,
Germany